FROM A HEAD,
THROUGH A HEAD,
TO A HEAD

FROM A HEAD, THROUGH A HEAD, TO A HEAD

THE SECRET CHANNEL BETWEEN THE US AND CHINA THROUGH PAKISTAN

F. S. Aijazuddin

OXFORD
UNIVERSITY PRESS

OXFORD

UNIVERSITY PRESS

Great Clarendon Street, Oxford OX2 6DP

Oxford University Press is a department of the University of Oxford.
It furthers the University's objective of excellence in research, scholarship,
and education by publishing worldwide in

Oxford New York

Athens Auckland Bangkok Bogotá Buenos Aires Calcutta
Cape Town Chennai Dar es Salaam Delhi Florence Hong Kong Istanbul
Karachi Kuala Lumpur Madrid Melbourne Mexico City Mumbai
Nairobi Paris São Paulo Shanghai Singapore Taipei Tokyo Toronto Warsaw

with associated companies in Berlin Ibadan

Oxford is a registered trade mark of Oxford University Press
in the UK and in certain other countries

© F. S. Aijazuddin

The moral rights of the author have been asserted

First published 2000

ISBN 0 19 579449 4

Printed in Pakistan at
Mehran Printers, Karachi.
Published by
Ameena Saiyid, Oxford University Press
5-Bangalore Town, Sharae Faisal
PO Box 13033, Karachi-75350, Pakistan.

The author is grateful to the following publishers for permission to quote from selected material:

The Executors of the late Lord Saint Brides and C. Hurst & Co. (Publishers) Ltd., for Sir Morrice James (Lord Saint Brides), *Pakistan Chronicle*.

Faber and Faber Ltd. for Walter Isaacson, *Kissinger: A Biography*.

Ambassador Sultan M. Khan for *Memories & Reflections of a Pakistani Diplomat*.

Macmillan Publishers Ltd. for Richard Nixon, *Leaders*.

Mr William Burr and The National Security Archive, Washington for W. Burr (ed.), *The Kissinger Transcripts*.

Oxford University Press, Pakistan, for Iqbal Akhund, *Memoirs of a Bystander*; Herbert Feldman, *The End and the Beginning of Pakistan 1969-1971*; and Stanley Wolpert, *Zulfi Bhutto of Pakistan*.

The Rowman & Littlefield Publishing Group for John H. Holdridge, *Crossing the Divide*.

Sang-e-Meel Publications for Altaf Gauhar, *Ayub Khan: Pakistan's First Military Ruler*.

Time Warner Trade Publishing for Richard Nixon, *Memoirs of Richard Nixon*; and for Henry Kissinger, *White House Years*.

FOR

AMBASSADOR AGHA HILALY
(PAKISTAN'S AMBASSADOR TO THE US, 1966–1971)

WHO 'WELL SERVED' HIS COUNTRY

CONTENTS

CONTENTS

LIST OF PHOTOGRAPHS

ACKNOWLEDGEMENTS

I am deeply indebted to Mr Ali Yahya Khan, the son of the late President Agha M. Yahya Khan, for making available to me the file maintained by his father on the secret US–China contacts. Yahya Khan's crucial intermediacy resulted in the first and historic visit by Dr Henry Kissinger (then Assistant for National Security Affairs to President Nixon) to Beijing in July 1971.

I am particularly grateful to Mr William Burr, Analyst at the National Security Archive, Washington and editor of *The Kissinger Transcripts. The Top Secret Talks with Beijing and Moscow* (New York, 1998) for timely help and advice. The arrival in Lahore of his recently published book followed by an unexpected meeting with him three weeks later in the National Security Archive in Washington were important incentives for me to complete this overdue study of the Yahya papers. His comments on the manuscript have been more valuable than I can acknowledge adequately here.

I owe a brief but sincere word of thanks to Ambassador Howard B. Schaffer, former US Ambassador to Bangladesh, who pointed me in the direction of the National Security Archive, and similar gratitude to the staff of the NSA and the Gelman Library, George Washington University for their assistance.

My thanks are also due to Mr Sanaullah, Director, Ministry of Foreign Affairs, Islamabad, to Mr Zhang Shi Chuan, First Secretary, Embassy of the People's Republic of China, Islamabad, and to Ms Bonnie Gutman, Director, the American Center, Lahore, for providing biographical details on the Pakistani, Chinese and American diplomats respectively mentioned in the text. I am grateful similarly to Ambassador Sultan M. Khan, former Foreign Secretary of Pakistan, for responding promptly and openly to my queries, and to Ambassador Bashir Babar for his help despite a personal bereavement.

The name of Ambassador Agha Hilaly will occur many more times in this volume. On this page, however, I wish to acknowledge his considerable help in clarifying a number of points, on providing supplementary material including photographs, and above all in helping me obtain a deeper insight into the secret communications between the United States and the People's Republic of China, all of which passed through his capable hands. His tactful insistence, then as now, on remaining out of the limelight makes it difficult to provide the full measure of his personal role in these sensitive negotiations. I hope the dedication of this book to him will serve as one individual tribute to his lifetime of discreet and self-effacing diplomacy.

To my darling wife Shahnaz, for all her unstinting love and support, my own love and deepest gratitude—from a heart to a heart.

EDITORIAL NOTE

Bibliographical references have been abbreviated to the name of the author and the year of publication.

The spelling of Chinese names have been retained as they appear in the original correspondence. Text references follow the modernised Pinyin system.

PREFACE

The core of this book consists of forty-nine secret documents from a file marked 'The Chinese Connection' assembled and maintained personally by the late President Yahya Khan of Pakistan. The documents cover the period 15 October 1969 to 7 August 1971, and include the messages sent by President Nixon and Dr Henry Kissinger to Premier Zhou Enlai through President Yahya, and vice versa.

The method used by them was that any messages from the White House were either dictated or typed on unmarked plain paper and handed personally to Mr Agha Hilaly,[1] Ambassador of Pakistan in Washington. He would then type the oral message or transcribe it in his own hand. The message would then be sent by diplomatic bag (or on one rare occasion by special courier) through the Foreign Secretary in Islamabad for delivery to President Yahya Khan, wherever he happened to be at the time. The Chinese response was communicated by the Chinese Ambassador in Islamabad to President Yahya privately. Yahya would have these transcribed and sent by his Military Secretary through the Foreign Office to Ambassador Agha Hilaly in Washington for delivery to the White House. Some messages, usually acknowledgements of receipt or of despatch, were sent by using the Foreign Office cypher.

Dr Kissinger, in his memoirs, imbues this clandestine flow of communication with a dramatic, almost transcendental quality: 'Hilaly said he was not authorized to leave the document with me. He therefore had to dictate it, speaking slowly as I copied it down. We were so preoccupied with this mechanical chore that we did not notice the incongruity of this elegant spokesman of the elite of a country based on an ancient religion dictating a communication from the leader of a militant Asiatic revolutionary nation to a representative of the leader of the Western capitalist world; or the phenomenon that in an age of instantaneous communication we had returned to the diplomatic methods of the previous century—the hand-written note delivered by messenger and read aloud. An event of fundamental importance took place in a pedantic, almost pedestrian, fashion.'[2]

The pragmatic reason for such a furtive procedure was the insistence by both the Americans and the Chinese for absolute secrecy. Neither of them, especially the White House, wanted any disclosure of what was a bold, daring but dangerous initiative between two declared adversaries. Once the secret channel became public knowledge, both could own up to it, and on occasion even laugh about it. For example, in an exchange during a meeting between Chairman Mao Zedong and Dr Kissinger (then Secretary of State) in Beijing on 12 November 1973, the Chinese leader chided Kissinger:

Chairman Mao: Yes. People say that Americans can keep no secrets.

Secretary Kissinger: That's true.

Chairman Mao: I think Americans can very well keep secrets.

Secretary Kissinger: That's basically true, Mr. Chairman, but you may be sure that as long as we keep the information in the White House, you can be sure that nothing has ever come out of our discussions.

Chairman Mao: Take the Cuban incident, for instance. Take for instance, your visit to China. And another situation would be your recent dealing with the Soviet Union. In all these cases, secrets were kept quite well.

Secretary Kissinger: That's true. Things we can keep in my office, we can keep quite well.[3]

The recent publication of transcripts like this one of meetings between Dr Kissinger and Chinese and Russian leaders has provided a deeper, often corrective dimension to the one-sided accounts contained in Kissinger's volumes of memoirs—*White House Years* (1979) and *Years of Upheaval* (1982), and to President Nixon's earlier and necessarily abridged account of the same events in *The Memoirs of Richard Nixon* (1978).

Reading their separate accounts, one is continuously aware of a simmering tension throughout the tortuous collaboration between the President and his subordinate. Although Nixon and Kissinger shared common ideals on how the world could be made a safer place for all mankind and even though they conceived as if with one mind the idea of triangular diplomacy with US, Russian and Chinese interests as three balancing counterpoints, they implemented their joint policy often conspiratorially using 'back channels' in their communications with world leaders to the exclusion of the US State Department and other Government agencies. Between themselves—despite the closeness of their collaboration—they remained intense and obdurate rivals.

It would be tempting to analogise their relationship as being that of a modern James Boswell and his mentor Dr Samuel Johnson. Although Nixon being the President could and did on occasions behave like the Johnson in their relationship, Dr Kissinger was determined to be his own Boswell. To achieve this, he took extraordinary pains to ensure control over his official papers. Even while in office, in early 1973, when he was on the brink of resigning from Nixon's second administration, he despatched thirty crates of documents to a bomb shelter in the Pocantico Hills estate of his benefactor Nelson Rockefeller.[4]

When finally he did leave the State Department in January 1977, Kissinger 'transferred to the Library of Congress copies of his White House and State Department files as part of a larger collection of his papers. Under his deed of gift to the Library, Kissinger retained access to them for writing his memoirs but exempted them from public access until 2001 or five years after his death, whichever occurred later.'[5]

Had Kissinger succeeded in covering his archives with the same tarpaulin of secrecy as he had his contacts with the Chinese in the years leading up to his visit to Beijing in July 1971, his memoirs would have enjoyed the same singular gravity of the Authorized Version of modern history. The recently published transcripts of Kissinger's talks with the Chinese and Soviet leadership, as edited by William Burr, have in a sense become an equivalent of the Dead Sea Scrolls; they serve as newly discovered touchstones of a previously unquestioned scripture. Through these transcripts, we receive different perceptions of the public figures than the ones they preferred to project. For example, we discover President Nixon telling Premier Zhou Enlai that, after the re-election he expected to win in 1972 (he did, with a landslide of 60.7 per cent of the popular vote), he would retain Dr Kissinger with him: 'He can't afford to stay, and I cannot afford to have him leave, because the book he would write would tell too much.'

Premier Zhou, who as Mao Zedong's shadow understood the invidiousness of Kissinger's position only too well, gently reminded Kissinger of his obligation to history: 'Yes, if it is your wish to promote the normalization of relations between China and the United States and if you left before fulfilling the mission, just to write a mere book, that would not be in accord with your philosophy.'

Dr Kissinger responded by asserting that he would stay with the President as long as the President thought he could be of service, adding that he did not intend 'to write a book at any event.' Nixon good-naturedly deigned to say that he would authorize Kissinger to write a book 'but he must write poetry.' Kissinger deflected the jibe with the self-effacing retort: 'Because of my Germanic origin, it would be of 400 pages.'[6]

Kissinger stayed with Nixon until the calamitous end of his Presidency. On 7 August 1974, just over three years after Kissinger's visit to Beijing, the two architects of the US–China détente found themselves alone again in the Oval Office, this time under tragically different circumstances. Nixon had decided to resign and Kissinger had been called by Alexander Haig, White House Chief of Staff, to mitigate the trauma.

"History will treat you more kindly than your contemporaries," Kissinger told him.

"It depends on who writes the history," retorted Nixon.[7]

In time both Nixon and Kissinger wrote their own separate versions of the history they made together. Of the two other contributors to the dramatic events which brought the United States and China closer—Premier Zhou Enlai of the People's Republic of China and President Yahya

Khan of Pakistan—neither left a comparable record of their participation in this historic conciliation. The Chinese Premier—in many ways, despite his espousal of Communism, the modern incarnation of a mandarin—was content to let destiny be his scribe. Cultured, unfailingly polite and sagacious, he knew that everything he said or did was transforming itself into history. He did not feel a need to articulate his version of it. As Thomas Carlyle had written in *Sartor Resartus*: 'Speech is of time, silence is of eternity'.[8]

Yahya Khan, having been ousted in December 1971 following the debacle in East Pakistan, chose to remain quiet all the time he was in 'protective custody' until his death in 1980. Yahya Khan was reticent about his role in the establishment of the Chinese connection, I suspect, because he expected these documents to testify for him, as I hope they do in the following pages. His failings as a military and political leader of Pakistan during the most traumatic period of its history in 1971, resulting in the bloody after-birth of the state of Bangladesh are all too well known. His role as the US–China interlocutor demands and deserves to be revealed. The following excerpt of the conversation between President Nixon and Premier Zhou Enlai—the best judges of his singular input—testify to the significance of his contribution:

> *Premier Zhou*: Both of us owe something to Yahya, although he did not show much statesmanship in leading his country, for bringing the link between our two countries.

> *President Nixon*: He is a bridge.

> *Premier Zhou*: We should not forget and we cannot forget, especially that Dr. Kissinger was able through him to come

secretly for talks here. And when a man makes a contribution to the world, we should remember him.[9]

The late President Yahya Khan would have preferred that, above all, as his epitaph.

F. S. Aijazuddin
Lahore,
December 1999

NOTES

1. Mr Agha Hilaly (born 1911) joined the Pakistan Foreign Service in September 1947. He served as Pakistan's ambassador to Sweden (1956–59), USSR (1959-61), India (1961) and to the United States (1966–71).
2. Kissinger (1979), p. 701.
3. Burr (1998), pp. 182–183.
4. Isaacson (1992), p. 231.
5. Burr (1998), pp. x–xi.
6. *Memorandum of Conversation No. 3,* 23 February 1972 (National Security Archive, Washington). Kissinger's first volume of memoirs *White House Years* runs to almost 1500 pages.
7. Quoted in Isaacson (1992), p. 597.
8. *Sartor Resartus: The Life and Opinions of Herr Teufelsdrockh* by Thomas Carlyle (1795–1881).
9. *Memorandum of Conversation No. 3,* 23 February 1972 (National Security Archive, Washington).

INTRODUCTION

In the summer of 1969, two journeys commenced from the United States. Both were fraught with hazard and required an inordinate amount of skill and courage to complete, both put the reputation of their country of origin at incalculable risk, and in the end, by following tightly controlled flight paths, both journeys reached a spectacular conclusion. After they were over, each would be acknowledged as a pioneering moment in history when man's perception of outer space and of his relationship with other men on our own planet changed direction, irreversibly.

The first was the journey of Apollo XI, which enabled two American astronauts—representatives of their country and of mankind—to reach and walk on the distant moon. The second was a journey begun by a President of the United States in July 1969 and completed by his chosen emissary exactly two years later, in July 1971. This latter voyage was towards the remote, diplomatically isolated People's Republic of China. That both achievements should have occurred during the presidency of Richard Nixon must be one of the enduring ironies of twentieth century politics, for the Apollo space exploration programme had been the dream-child not of Nixon but of his predecessor and rival John F. Kennedy, and no one expected Nixon—an avowed communist-baiter[1]—to establish the first significant contact between the capitalist United States and the Communist People's Republic of China.

Exactly when Nixon stopped seeing red is not known. Certainly a month after his inauguration in January 1969, Nixon, now President and at par with the French president Charles de Gaulle,[2] gave form during his discussions with him in Paris to the incubus of an idea that China could no longer be excluded from the international community and that he, as the president of the United States, was probably the only person with the unquestionable power and therefore the credibility to make such an admissive gesture.

Exchanging ideas on global matters with de Gaulle, Nixon steered the conversation towards China. 'As we talked,' he wrote in his *Memoirs*, 'I could see that his thinking paralleled my own. "I have no illusions about their ideology," he said, "but I do not feel that we should leave them isolated in their rage. The West should try to get to know China, to have contacts, and to penetrate it."

Nixon prevaricated, admitting that the West might find China a useful counter in their dealings with the Soviet bloc: 'In ten years, when China has made significant progress, we will have no choice.'

De Gaulle replied, with the weight of wisdom: "It would be better for you to recognize China before you are obliged to do so by the growth of China".[3]

Later in the same year, after his meeting with de Gaulle, Nixon embarked on a world trip, code named Moonglow. He flew to the South Pacific to welcome the returning Apollo XI astronauts, and then, travelling through the Far East, he visited Pakistan making a twenty-two hour stopover in Lahore on 1 August 1969.

At the banquet given for him and Mrs Nixon by President Yahya Khan at Governor's House that evening, Nixon recalled having been to Pakistan twice as Vice President and twice more in a private capacity, and then, using a remark made by one of the guests to him soon after his arrival, he said 'that on this occasion, our stay in Pakistan would be exactly 22 hours, which happens to coincide with the exact number of hours that the two astronauts spent on the moon.'[4]

Nixon spent some of the twenty-two hours encouraging Yahya Khan to act as an intermediary with the Chinese leadership on his behalf. For this, Yahya Khan needed no prompting. While still C-in-C of the Pakistan army, he had such a contact with Premier Zhou Enlai during one of their meetings in Beijing. He recalled later: 'He wouldn't give me a proper reply. He'd only say: "You'll hear from me." And no sooner had I reached Pindi than I received a message from Zhou that it was all right to go ahead and open negotiations on his behalf.'[5]

From Pakistan, Nixon flew to Romania, where he had an identical discussion with President Nicolae Ceaucescu,[6] encouraging him also to open a dialogue of contact with the Chinese. That the Romanian leader would inevitably disclose such information to his Soviet allies was anticipated by Nixon. For some time therefore, Nixon used both channels—the soft-capitalist Pakistani and the soft-communist Romanian—as parallel conduits of his policy.

If Nixon's political de-coloration had been a gradual process, precipitated after he came to power, the conversion of the man he chose as his solo astronaut on the flight to China was equally dramatic. Like most patriotic Americans at the time—especially if they were former émigrés from Nazi Germany—Henry Kissinger shared the view that Communism was an evil which, if it could not be eradicated, ought at least to be contained. Unlike his colleagues, though, he saw the possibility of accentuating schisms between the Soviets and the Chinese, to the advantage of the West.

Ideological and other differences had already begun to develop between the two Communist monoliths, separating them to an extent that China felt that it was threatened militarily by Russia as much as it was by the West. Kissinger noted: 'I was encouraged in late January [1970] when I read a report of a conversation between Chinese Premier Chou En-lai and the Pakistani Ambassador in Peking. The Ambassador found Chou En-lai primarily concerned about the Soviet Union, secondarily about the revival of Japanese militarism. As for the United States, Chou clearly considered it a lesser threat; he seemed quite prepared for high-level talks with the United States, provided we took the initiative. In fact, according to this report, Chou En-lai mused about our apparent unwillingness "to take a step like Kosygin"—in other words, to send a high official to Peking.'[7]

This feeling of vulnerability to attack was repeated to Kissinger by Zhou Enlai when they finally met in July 1971. Kissinger reported to Nixon that 'China professed apprehension over the possibility that the US, USSR, Japan and even India might collaborate to carve up China. He showed deep bitterness against the Soviets and contempt for their petty tactics.'[8]

Zhou alluded to China's feelings of insecurity yet again when he met Nixon on 22 February 1972: 'The worst possibility is ...the eventuality that you all would attack China—the Soviet Union comes from the north, Japanese and the U.S. from the east, and India into China's Tibet.'[9] China saw itself, Zhou told Kissinger, not as a superpower at par with either the United States of America or Russia but as a champion of 'less powerful' countries. It wished to avoid the 'vice of great power ambitions which have only served to stir turmoil in the world and brought problems for the powers themselves.'[10]

This theme surfaced again during discussions on 12 November 1973 between Kissinger, by then promoted to Secretary of State, and the Chinese leaders Chairman Mao Zedong and Zhou Enlai. Exchanging views in Mao's residence in Beijing in that winter evening, Kissinger made an unusual disclaimer:

Secretary Kissinger: ...The Soviet Union like to create the impression that they and we have a master plan to run the world, but that is to trap other countries. It's not true. We are not that foolish.

Chairman Mao: You are always saying with respect to the Soviet Union something we are ourselves always saying. And your views seem approximately the same as ours, that is, there is a possibility that the Soviet Union wants to attack China.

Secretary Kissinger: Well, Mr. Chairman, I used to think of it as a theoretical possibility. Now I think it is more a realistic possibility, and I've said it, especially to your Prime Minister and also your Ambassador. I think they above all want to destroy your nuclear capability.

Chairman Mao: But our nuclear capability is no bigger than a fly of this size.

Secretary Kissinger: But they are worried about what it will be ten years from now.

Chairman Mao: I'd say thirty years hence or fifty years hence. And it is impossible for a country to rise up in a short period.

Secretary Kissinger: Well, as I have said...we believe that if this eventuality were to happen, it would have very serious consequences for everybody. And we are determined to oppose it as our own decision without any arrangement with China.

[Mao's response was less philosophical than prophetic.]

Chairman Mao: Their ambitions are contradictory with their capacity.[11]

From the Chinese side their receptivity to any sort of contact with the United States was conditioned by their experience of previous American Presidents. Mao felt no qualms about sharing his opinions about Nixon's predecessors with him when they met on 21 February 1972, nor about referring to him in the third person in his presence. The transcript reads:

Chairman Mao: The former President of Pakistan introduced President Nixon to us. At that time, our Ambassador in Pakistan refused to agree on our having a contact with you. He said it should be compared whether President Johnson or President Nixon would be better. But President Yahya said the two men cannot be compared, that these two men are incomparable. He said that one was like a gangster—he meant President Johnson. I don't know how he got that impression. We on our side were not very happy with that President either. We were not happy with your former Presidents, beginning from Truman through Johnson. We were not very happy with these Presidents, Truman and Johnson.

In between there were eight years of a Republican President. During that period probably you hadn't thought things out either.

Prime Minister Zhou: The main thing was John Foster Dulles' policy.[12]

[That John Foster Dulles,[13] a former Secretary of State during the 1950s, should have surfaced during the discussions between Mao and Nixon is an indication of how deeply rooted Chinese resentment had remained at Dulles' unconscionable refusal to shake Zhou's outstretched hand when they encountered each other at the 1954 Geneva Conference on Indochina. Both Nixon and Kissinger attempted separately to heal that hurt when they met Zhou by deliberately being seen to extend a hand to him before he did.[14]]

Continuing the discussions, Mao then threw the ball in Dr Kissinger's direction, asking him whether he had anything to add. Kissinger responded by saying: 'Mr. Chairman, the world situation has also changed dramatically during that period. We've had to learn a great deal. We thought all socialist/communist states were the same phenomenon. We didn't understand until the President came into office the different nature of revolution in China and the way revolution had developed in other socialist states.'[15] Dr Kissinger's analysis encapsulated the altered perceptions of global movements and changes which the United States felt impelled to understand and to come to negotiating terms with.

If Nixon put his plan of a rapprochement with China into motion in mid 1969, it took Mao a full year to respond to the overture. In the late summer of 1970, Mao 'startled party leaders when he told them about the secret communications with Washington and his acceptance of a U.S. proposal for a visit by one of its representatives'.[16] Meanwhile he toyed with those foreign visitors who did call on him, asking them as he did Mr Arshad Hussain, Pakistan's Foreign Minister: "Aren't you worried to be meeting a well-known bandit, and an infamous guerrilla leader. Isn't that how the Americans describe me?"[17]

Surprisingly for one who had such a vast understanding of global issues and contemporary events and who, according to his personal physician, loved to travel,[18] Mao Zedong had rarely stepped outside China. Yet he remained abreast of what was happening in a world which gradually and grudgingly accorded him the place destiny had already bestowed on him. Andre Malraux, the French writer and savant, talked to Mao about things which perhaps no Chinese would have dared—about his mortality, succession, and his place in history. Malraux later told Nixon: 'I once asked him if he did not think himself as the heir of the last great Chinese emperors of the sixteenth century. Mao said, "But of course, I am the heir".'[19] This explains why Mao, when Nixon met him at last, could deflect his compliment that Mao's writings 'moved a nation and have changed the world,' with the imperial reproof: 'I haven't been able to change it. I've only been able to change a few places in the vicinity of Beijing.'[20]

If Mao was the emperor in proletarian clothes, Zhou Enlai was the quintessential courtier within a Mao jacket. Diligent, extremely hardworking, obedient, attentive and always deferential to his superior, Zhou was prepared to leave visitors whom he accompanied into Mao's presence with the impression that he merely reflected like the moon the radiance of Mao's sun-like brilliance. Many who knew both Zhou Enlai and Kissinger remarked on the contrast between the two, usually in favour of Zhou. (Henry Kissinger had once been described by a former acolyte as 'the typical product of an authoritarian background—devious with his peers, domineering with his subordinates, obsequious to his superiors.'[21])

Almost a quarter of a century in age separated Zhou Enlai from his younger American counterpart. That he was able to bridge also the political and cultural chasm dividing them was a tribute to his sagacity, wisdom and radial foresight.

Zhou Enlai had studied for a while in Germany during the 1920s, as indeed Kissinger had done before migrating to the US in 1938. Zhou had also spent time in France before returning to China where he became involved in the freedom struggle. He may have studied in Europe but all the lessons he needed were those he learned during the harrowing and subsequently legendary Long March in 1934 from Kiangsi to Shensi, over 6,000 miles away. After the establishment of the People's Republic of China, he was propelled into the premiership which he held until his death in 1976.

Holding the additional responsibility of Foreign Minister, Zhou, during his long and distinguished career, represented his fledgling government's interests in numerous international forums, most conspicuously at the Afro-Asian Conference of non-aligned nations convened at Bandung in April 1955. It was the first such major congregation of leaders from the emergent Third World, all of whom—notably Sukarno, Tito, Nasser, Zhou and Nehru—represented a post-war population of mini-powers who had shaken free of their colonial or war-worn shackles but not yet found their feet.

Nehru, according to the interpretation of his biographer Sarvepalli Gopal, relied upon the trust and goodwill generated by his own visit to China in October 1954. He saw a role for himself at the Bandung conference 'as a producer-manager rather than as a hero; and had he not willingly abdicated, Chou would not have been the central figure. If Chou appeared to be the star of Bandung, frequently timing his diplomatic operations so as to overshadow the India Prime Minister, Nehru regarded Chou's success as his own personal triumph.'[22]

At Bandung, Zhou also met the Pakistani Prime Minister M.A. Bogra.[23] They exchanged invitations to visit each other's countries. Zhou appreciated that Pakistan had been one of the first countries in the world to recognise on 4 January 1950 the People's Republic of China, and although this act of support was vitiated to a degree by Pakistan four years later when it joined SEATO—perceived by the Chinese as a US sponsored girdle of containment— relations at the formal level continued to remain mutually cordial. Zhou's invitation to Bogra was used by the next prime minister, H.S. Suhrawardy[24] who visited Beijing in October 1956. Premier Zhou reciprocated by paying a visit to Pakistan, his reception at Dacca being regarded by a well-meaning but careless scribe as 'a watermark in Sino– Pakistan relations.'

Soon after Bandung, China apparently sent a message to Pakistan assuring its government that 'there was no conceivable clash of interests between the two countries which could imperil their friendly relations: but that this position did not apply to Indo-Chinese relations, in which a definite conflict of interests could be expected in the near future.'[25] It hinted of an incipient clash between the Indians and the Chinese. The conflict erupted in 1962, when the determined Chinese overran poorly equipped Indian troops in the Ladakh area. 'There were clashes between Chinese and Indian troops in the western part of Sinkiang, the Ak-sai Chin area,' Zhou Enlai told Nixon and Kissinger later. 'In that part of Sinkiang province there is a high plateau. The Indian-occupied territory was at the foot of the Karakorums, and the disputed territory was on the slope between.'

"It's what they call Ladakh," Dr. Kissinger added.

"They attacked up the mountain," Nixon said.

Zhou continued: 'We fought them and beat them back, with many wounded. But the TASS agency said that China had committed aggression against India.'[26]

The Chinese leadership held India, encouraged by the Soviet Union, to be the aggressors. Zhou Enlai felt betrayed by what he believed to be Khrushchev's insidious stand. He contested with vehemence the specious logic of the Soviet leader that the number of casualties could be used as the barometer of innocence. 'He [Khrushchev] said: "The casualties on the Indian side were greater than yours, so that's why I believe they were victims of aggression." If the side with the most casualties is to be considered the victim of aggression, what logic would that be? For example, at the end of the Second World War, Hitler's troops were all casualties or taken prisoner, and that means that Hitler was the victim of aggression.'[27]

There are a number of published accounts of the Sino–Indian conflict. The one which the Chinese thought presented the situation (and their point of view) most fairly was Neville Maxwell's *India's China War*.[28] Nixon deliberately referred to this book during his frosty meeting with Mrs Indira Gandhi in the Oval Office in 1971, commenting that it was 'a very interesting account of the beginning of the war between India and China'. Zhou laughed when he heard that 'she didn't react very favorably' to that.[29]

The relevance of that war was two fold: it shattered India's illusions about China and their ability to collaborate as fraternal equals ('*Hindi-Chini, bhai-bhai*') against the major power blocs, and secondly, it made India disagreeably aware of China's superior prowess, of its own military weaknesses, and of the necessity to choose one's opponents relative to size.

In neighbouring Pakistan, which had common borders with both India and China, democratically elected but fragile governments had been replaced by the military leadership of General Ayub Khan, initially as Chief Martial Law Administrator in 1958 and later as President from 1962. Ayub Khan began his rule with military no-nonsense precision, and saw the advantage of achieving an understanding with China on such contentious issues as the definition of national boundaries. It seems strange, almost negligent, that nations which were created on paper by the stroke of a pen should not have known, even fifteen years after their creation, what their borders actually were on the ground—until one remembers that in one inflammable case, that of Kashmir, even fifty years has not been long enough.

Boundary negotiations began between Pakistan and China on 3 May 1962, and within ten months, by 2 March 1963, these negotiations had been completed and the Sino–Pakistan Boundary Agreement signed, defining the boundary between Sinkiang Province and that part of Kashmir under Pakistan's control.[30] Zulfikar Ali Bhutto, Ayub Khan's mercurial Foreign Minister claimed credit for the achievement. Stung by the Indian accusation that he had conceded areas that did not belong to Pakistan in the first place, Bhutto hotly denied that he had given away even 'a single inch'. Quite the contrary, he argued, he had in fact gained 750 square miles of territory 'which had till then been in China's occupation and control.'[31] According to an official bulletin, 'the Pak-China border thus became "a border of peace and tranquility".'[32]

With the Russians siding with India against China it would have been bad politics for China and Pakistan not to have moved closer. Zulfikar Ali Bhutto, as Foreign Minister, visited Beijing in March 1963, his gesture being reciprocated by Zhou Enlai who paid his second visit to Pakistan, staying in the country between 18–26 February 1964. Ayub Khan tried to emulate the sort of reception the Chinese could muster for foreign dignitaries. The streets were lined with schoolchildren and smartly uniformed troops who guarded the long road from the airport to Karachi's city centre. What he could not control was the gaucherie of the private sector. Proud of the strides Pakistan was taking towards industrialisation, Ayub Khan arranged for Premier Zhou Enlai to be shown around one of Karachi's largest textile factories. Sir Morrice James, the British High Commissioner, who was among the guests, describes how the function went awry: 'Later Chou and his party visited Dawood Mills, with their owner as guide. Dawood[33] had recently begun improving the lot of his workers by introducing various welfare schemes, and he described them to Chou, ending as was his custom with a resounding declaration that if other employers would follow his lead there would be no danger of the industrial workforce turning to Communism. Chou received this statement with appropriate inscrutability.'[34]

On a more serious note, Sir Morrice evaluated the benefit Pakistan had derived from Premier Zhou's visit: 'Thus the Pakistanis secured some useful gains from the visit at gratifyingly low political cost. The formula about Kashmir used in the communiqué suited their book well. More important, they had managed to achieve a fairly friendly relationship with one of the two principal Communist powers, without China having demanded, as the Soviet Union did, that Pakistan should first drop its membership of SEATO and CENTO.' He concluded: 'It seemed after all that he [Ayub] was just as skilful at playing the non-aligned game as the Indians who had invented it.'[35]

Meanwhile, earlier in August 1963, an Air Agreement had been signed between China and Pakistan, as a result of which Pakistan International Airlines became the first non-Communist airline to start a service with regular international flights between Dacca-Canton-Shanghai. The United States Government retaliated by suspending a loan for the renovation of Dacca airport.

It is an arguable point whether the Sino–Indian war of 1962 should be viewed as the crucible for the subsequent conflict in 1965 between India and Pakistan. Like that earlier conflict, though, it had the effect of winnowing the wheat of friendship from the chaff of paper alliances. Predictably, Russia sided with India, and China came to the aid of Pakistan. The position of the United States was conditioned by its realization of India's growing importance as a regional power and of Pakistan's pretentious and unseemly familiarity with China.

When in 1960, Bhutto, for example, as the leader of Pakistan's delegation to the UN voted against the US sponsored blockade of China from that body, the reaction from Washington through the then Foreign Minister Manzur Qadir was swift and specific. Bhutto's 'discretionary powers' on future UN votes were peremptorily withdrawn.[36]

Later, in 1963, when Bhutto had gone to Washington to represent Pakistan at the assassinated President John Kennedy's funeral, 'President Johnson made no secret of his displeasure at the new turn in Pakistan's foreign policy and took Bhutto personally to task for Pakistan's growing closeness to China and his personal contacts with Sukarno'.[37]

Bhutto took cold comfort from the fact that the initiatives he fathered matured with Kissinger's dramatic visit to Beijing in July 1971. Writing as Prime Minister of the residual Pakistan he helped amputate to a proportion manageable by him alone, he complained: 'It is ironical that the correctness of Pakistan's policy towards China was vindicated for the United States by subsequent developments in the world situation [.] As far back as 1965–66, I had conveyed to President Johnson and Secretary of State Rusk[38] that Pakistan could serve as a bridge between China and the United States. When, in a conversation I had with Dean Rusk in Ankara, this possibility was explored, Ayub Khan took alarm and said that we should not "burn our fingers". More than fingers were burnt when, in 1971—five crucial destructive years after I had first put forth the proposition—Yahya Khan's regime made arrangements for Dr. Kissinger to fly through Pakistan on his secret mission to Peking.'[39]

Ayub Khan's relationship with his talented but irascible Foreign Minister had none of the consistency of Mao Zedong's with his Foreign Minister Zhou Enlai. If anything it was closer to the tempestuous one between Nixon and his troublesome assistant Kissinger. If Nixon had a war in Vietnam and Kissinger on his hands, he had the consolation of knowing that he could use one to end the other. Ayub Khan too had a war and a testy subordinate on his hands. His compensation was that he did not need Bhutto to end his war. To him, Bhutto was dispensable even if he did threaten him as a political alternative.

In a recent biography of Ayub Khan, Altaf Gauhar, his former Minister of Information, disclosed how, during the course of the 1965 war, Ayub Khan panicked and appealed for help from US President Lyndon B. Johnson. On being rebuffed, he flew to China during the night of 19–20 September, to consult with the Chinese leadership. Accompanied by Mr Bhutto, he met Premier Zhou and Marshal Chen Yi. The published exchange between them makes sad reading for those generations affected by that war:

> Ayub explained the military situation and how the Indians, because of their superiority in numbers, were beginning to strengthen their hold, and how western powers were giving full diplomatic support to India while persuading the Soviet Union to assume the role of the mediator. Chou En-lai said that numerical superiority would be of no avail to the Indians in a prolonged war. Even if one or two major cities were lost, the Pakistani forces, supported by a patriotic people, could inflict crippling blows on the invaders. He recalled instances from China's long struggle for liberation to show that numerical superiority cannot prevail on the will of the people. Ayub explained that the flat terrain of the Punjab was not suitable for mounting guerrilla attacks on an advancing enemy. Marshal Chen Yi intervened to say that every little canal, every bit of high ground could be used as cover. Chou En-lai said: "And don't forget that we will be maintaining our pressure all the time." Ayub asked: "How long would you maintain the pressure?" Chou En-lai looked straight into Ayub's eyes and said, "For as long as necessary, but you must keep fighting, even if you have to withdraw to the hills." Ayub did not know how to respond to this offer of unconditional support. He said: "Mr. Prime Minister, I think you are being rash." Chou En-lai smiled and cautioned Ayub against succumbing to American pressure: "And don't fall into the Russian trap. They are unreliable. You will find out the truth." Ayub tried to reassure Chou En-lai that Pakistan was China's friend: "I am not going to turn like Nehru. Please convey this to Chairman Mao." By the end it became clear that if Pakistan wanted full Chinese support it had to be prepared for a long war in which some major cities like Lahore might be lost. However, every reverse would unite the people and the Indian forces would be sucked into a quagmire of popular resistance. Neither Ayub nor Bhutto was prepared for this. The whole Foreign Office strategy was

designed as a quick-fix to force the Indians to the negotiating table. Ayub had never foreseen the possibility of the Indians surviving a couple of hard blows, and Bhutto had never envisaged a long drawn out people's war. Above all, the Army and the Air Force were totally against any further prolongation of the conflict.[40]

Much to the private mortification of the Chinese, the warring pugilists were drawn apart by the Russian Premier Alexei Kosygin. The fighting was brought to an abrupt end, and at Tashkent, on 10 January 1966, President Ayub Khan and Indian Prime Minister Lal Bahadur Shastri signed a joint Declaration confirming their 'firm resolve to restore normal and peaceful relations between their countries', to observe the cease-fire, and to withdraw to positions they started from on 5 August 1965, when hostilities had broken out. The fallout of Tashkent, like that of Chernobyl, wafted over history. Among its more notable casualties was the Indian prime minister Shastri who died during the night, Bhutto who was removed from the Foreign Ministry after six months, and Ayub Khan who was eased out of the presidency three years later.

Whatever lessons the Pakistan Army had learned and whatever advice Zhou Enlai and Marshal Chen Yi had given to Ayub Khan during the course of the 1965 war were, however, soon forgotten. When another military delegation—this time of a lower level—accompanying Mr Ghulam Faruque, Commerce Minister, called on Zhou Enlai in August 1966, the Chinese Premier would have been forgiven for being overcome by a sense of *deja vu*. Ambassador Sultan M. Khan described the scene:

On the final day of their stay in Beijing the Delegation was received by Chou En-lai. He said all the requirements on their list would be met and that the timing of deliveries would soon be intimated, but cautioned that due to the pressing needs of Vietnam, some items on Pakistan's list would be subject to delay. He then remarked that he had seen our list but was not clear in his mind on what basis the quantity of ammunition had been calculated.

One of the Generals replied that these were based on fourteen days' reserve supplies, which prompted Chou En-lai to ask, "And what happens after fourteen days? How can a war be fought in that short a time?"

The General explained that Pakistan hoped that during that time, the Security Council would meet and call upon both parties to the conflict to cease-fire and withdraw armed forces to their respective borders.

"Please forgive me," Chou En-lai said, "if I appear to be confused by your reply. But is the outcome of a conflict has been predetermined to be a restoration of the *status quo ante*, then why fight after all? Why unnecessarily waste human lives and economic resources? Wars cannot be fought according to a time-table, and one has to be ready for a prolonged conflict." There was no answer from our side.

"As your friend," Chou En-lai continued, "I would be interested to know if any of you have prepared the people of Pakistan to operate in the rear of the enemy, in the event of your first line of defence being broken, to cut the enemy's lines of communications, disrupt his supplies and generally inflict damage. I am talking about a People's Militia being based in every village and town. Since Pakistan lacks an industrial base to replenish supplies, this kind of defence is obviously well suited to its needs."

There was a stunned silence among the Generals. The concept of putting arms into the hands of the common man was totally alien to them; in fact, it seemed a threat to law and order in Pakistan. The notion of a prolonged conflict involving the citizenry of Pakistan was not part of the defence strategy planned by these professional soldiers.

Chou En-lai next brought up his favourite tactical theme, which the P.L.A. had practiced successfully during the civil and anti-Japanese wars.

Instead of placing a defensive line to match the enemy at every point, why not, he asked, open a gap somewhere, draw the enemy to a pre-selected position, then surround him and wipe him out? Clenching a fist, Chou En-lai said, "*This* is capable of delivering a forceful blow, but if you cut off one finger, the fist loses its power, not by one-fifth, but by fifty per cent. If you wipe out a couple of hundred thousand of the enemy spread over a long front, its impact is not as great as wiping out an entire battalion or a brigade—the enemy's morale is dealt a devastating blow. We know this from practical experience."

Unfortunately, his words were not falling on receptive ears. The military doctrine taught at Staff College Quetta was inherited from the British—a great industrial power—and did not visualize unorthodox tactics better suited to a country lacking in any military-industrial capability.

When the generals met in my home for dinner that night they appeared to be upset, and one of them, tugging at the high collar of his uniform jacket, said: "War is a serious business and should be left to the professionals. Imagine a People's Militia! They would only mess up things and get in the way of the army." And he concluded by asking, "What does Chou En-lai know about soldiering and military affairs anyway?"

I was amazed by his ignorance, and surprised that he had not bothered to read the brief on Chou En-lai provided by the Embassy. So I reminded him that Chou En-lai had fought in more battles than one could count. For several years he was a Divisional Commander and then Chief of the General Staff of the People's Liberation Army.[41]

The Ambassador's behind-the-scenes record of this incident has been quoted *in extenso* as it is indicative of an attitude shown by many Pakistan governments towards its large and influential neighbour China. It has been said with a degree of truth that the Pakistanis love China for what it can do for them, while the Chinese love Pakistanis despite what they do to themselves. There could have no greater evidence of this aphorism than the economic and industrial support the Chinese continued to give to Pakistan during the second half of the 1960s, the disappointment of the failed 1965 war notwithstanding.

In October 1967, an agreement was signed to reopen the traditional overland route known as the Silk Route, which had been closed for over twenty years. A modern highway—a twentieth century concrete and macadam route—known as the Karakoram Highway or the broadway of friendship was completed in February 1971, linking Gilgit with Kashgar through the Khunjerab Pass. Two years later it was agreed to convert this into an international highway. Completed over twenty years with great ingenuity, effort and the loss of both Chinese and Pakistani lives, it was useable in 1978 and opened to the public in May 1986. A marvel of modern engineering, it has nearly 100 bridges, 1700 culverts and is wide enough to accommodate two tanks moving abreast in either direction.

Other major projects provided by the Chinese were the Heavy Mechanical Complex at Taxila, near the famous site visited by at least three ancient Buddhist pilgrims from China—Fa Hsien in 403, Sun Yung in 520 and Xuan Zang in 630 AD. Similarly, on the principle that if you can teach a man to fish, he should be able to feed himself, the Chinese provided Pakistan with assistance to establish an Ordnance factory in East Pakistan. It was completed and inaugurated in March 1970 by their Minister for Economic Relations Mr Fang Yi.

In addition, each year goodwill delegations were invited from Pakistan to participate in the celebrations for the founding of the People's Republic of China. In 1969, the delegation was headed by the Pakistan's Chief of Army Staff Lieutenant General Abdul Hamid Khan, and the following year by another army man, Lieutenant General Attiqur Rahman.

On the diplomatic front, at the United Nations Pakistan consistently supported China's application for membership, without palpable success. Even though China was able to secure a simple majority in 1971, it did not have a two-third majority and so again, for the twentieth time in twenty-one years, China found itself excluded from membership of the United Nations. China had become inured to such slights. Finally in 1971, the international community having, like Foster Dulles withheld its hand for twenty-seven unjustifiable years, extended it and welcomed the People's Republic of China into the comity of the United Nations. If that could be construed as a diplomatic triumph for China, it was in a smaller measure, silent praise for the supportive role Pakistan had played.

In a narrower sense, the role Pakistan played in assisting to deliver Dr Henry Kissinger to Beijing in July 1971 went similarly unsung. It was a service for which, as Kissinger said in his memoirs, he and Nixon 'as the only two senior officials who knew the facts were profoundly grateful'. He added: 'It was a service for which Pakistan's leaders, to their lasting honor, never sought any reciprocity or special consideration.'[42] One strident voice that would have disagreed, and did so in writing years later, was the Russian Foreign Minister Andrei Gromyko. Reviewing Russo–Pak relations and Pakistan's instinct to subordinate its own interests at the expense of its own independence, he commented caustically: 'It is truly amazing that they allow themselves to be used by others, as tools in a conflict that can only damage their own national interests.'[43] Before the year was out, Pakistan paid the price.

Credit for the historic initiative leading up to Kissinger's secret trip to Beijing was claimed both by Nixon and by Kissinger. That was to be expected. They were both temperamentally loners, secretive, less than forthcoming with others and with each other.[44] They knew that neither of them would have been able to achieve such a breakthrough alone. Fate had brought them together; their egos kept them apart. It is said that victory has a thousand fathers. In the case of the successful visit to Beijing by Kissinger, nature was less liberal. Its two sires fought a petty battle for custody.

Nixon dearly wanted to be the first American of his stature to visit Beijing. Kissinger managed to thwart that. Nixon tried to get Kissinger not to include his own name in the final communiqué. He failed. And so he hit back by having Kissinger 'sell' his qualities as a strong and forceful President. He had a list prepared at his own behest tabulating his attributes. They began with 'RN goes into such meetings better prepared than anyone who has ever held this office', and ended with a crafted image of the President of the United States strong enough to resist 'the temptation which was so obviously presented to him, particularly with the Chinese, of eating nuts and other goodies put before him'. Kissinger, on reading the list, thought some 'on the mark, others were bizarre.'[45] Zhou Enlai would have advised him to ignore it, as he had had to do in a similarly tactless situation in Karachi, with 'appropriate inscrutability'.

On the morning of 9 July 1971, Kissinger, tense but excited, cruising high over the highest mountains of the world, must have wondered at the lattice of paradoxes that had combined to take him on the journey to Beijing. He was travelling in a carrier owned by Pakistanis, manned by Pakistanis, on a visit planned through the offices of Pakistanis. He might have recalled his press conference at New Delhi airport nine years earlier when, asked about Pakistan's 'budding flirtation with China', he responded: 'I cannot imagine Pakistan doing such a foolish thing.'[46]

And further, he was doing so on behalf of a President who admired the drive of the Japanese and the Germans, but regretted that the 'people of the subcontinent, perhaps because of the environment, never had these qualities.'[47]

Born a Jew, Kissinger had consciously ignored the anti-Semitism feelings of his president, enduring them at the White House because, as he explained to his assistant Winston Lord: "I have enough trouble fighting with him on the things that really matter; his attitudes towards Jews and blacks are not my worry."[48]

He was going on a journey the likelihood of which he had himself discounted. When told that Nixon intended to visit China before the end of his second term, Kissinger had replied dismissively: "Fat chance."

The chance had come, and it had come to him.

As the PIA Boeing entered Chinese airspace, his assistant, Winston Lord, positioned himself forward in the aircraft so that he should be, technically at least, the first American official to cross into China. Neither fate nor Henry Kissinger was likely to be thwarted by such a simple stratagem. When, at fifteen minutes past noon on 9 July 1971, after the PIA plane landed at a military airport on the perimeters of Beijing, Kissinger emerged from the aircraft, walked down the gangway and stepped on communist Chinese territory.

It was a small step for an American diplomat, and a giant leap for international diplomacy.

NOTES

1. Richard Nixon's maiden speech in Congress on 18 February 1947 was to present 'a contempt of Congress citation against Gerhart Eisler, who had been identified as the top Communist agent in America.' He later worked for its Committee on Un-American Activities.

2. De Gaulle (1890–1970) was one of France's leading statesmen and war heroes. He was President for eleven years, between 1958–69, and responsible for France's withdrawal from Algeria and its other African colonies.

3. Nixon (1978), pp. 373–4. Also quoted in Nixon's essay on de Gaulle in his *Leaders* (1982), p. 74.

4. Reported in *Dawn*, 2 August 1969.

5. President Yahya Khan to author FSA, Rawalpindi, 2 August 1975. Some of Nixon's twenty-two hours in Lahore were spent without his host, who told him: 'In Pakistan, during the summer we have a custom. After lunch we rest. I propose to have a nap and I suggest, Mr. President, that you do the same.'

6. The first President of the Socialist Republic of Romania (1974–89), known for his pro-west inclinations.

7. Kissinger (1979), p. 687.

8. *Memorandum for the President from Henry A. Kissinger*, 17 July 1971, p. 19 (Record Group 59. Dept. of State Records, 1970–73). I am indebted to Mr William Burr of the National Security Archive, Washington, for drawing my attention to this Memorandum and for generously making a copy available.

9. *Memorandum of Conversation No. 2*, 22 February 1972, p.18 (National Security Archive, Washington).

10. Kissinger to Nixon, *Memorandum*, 17 July 1971, p. 19.

11. Burr (1998), p. 183.

12. Burr (1998), p. 63.

13. John F. Dulles (1888–1959), served as Secretary of State for six years (1953–59) during Eisenhower's presidency.

14. See Nixon (1978), p. 559 and Kissinger (1978), p. 742.

15. Burr (1998), pp. 63–4.

16. Burr (1998), p. 14.

17. Khan (1997), p. 209.

18. Li (1996), p. 128: 'Mao traveled constantly. He was rarely in Beijing.[...] He would travel for months at a time, returning to Beijing only for mandatory appearances on May Day and National Day and for visits with foreign guests.'
19. Malraux, quoted in Nixon (1978), p. 558.
20. Burr (1998), p. 60.
21. Leslie Gelb, quoted in Isaacson (1992), p. 100.
22. Gopal (1979), II, p. 241.
23. Mohammed Ali Bogra (Pakistan's third Prime Minister, 1953–55).
24. Huseyn Shaheed Suhrawardy (Pakistan's fourth Prime Minister, 1956–57).
25. Williams (1962), p. 120. The author L. F. Rushbrook Williams cites an 'unimpeachable authority' for this information.
26. *Memorandum of Conversation No. 3*, 23 February 1972, p. 3 (National Security Archive, Washington).
27. *Memorandum of Conversation No. 3*, 23 February 1972, p. 4 (National Security Archive, Washington).
28. Maxwell, Neville *India's China War* (London, 1970).
29. *Memorandum of Conversation No. 3*, 23 February 1972, p. 3 (National Security Archive, Washington).
30. 'Prime Minister Chou: We have [...] a non-disputed borderline with Bhutan, and later with Pakistan. Of course, this raised a problem with India, because they said the borderline included part of their territory.' *Memorandum of Conversation No. 3*, 23 February 1972, p. 25 (National Security Archive, Washington).
31. Wolpert (1993), p. 73.
32. *Pakistan Year Book 1969*, p. 126.
33. Mr Ahmed Dawood, one of Pakistan's leading textile magnates.
34. James (1993), p. 112.
35. James (1993), pp. 113–4.
36. Wolpert (1993), p. 65.
37. Akhund (1997), p. 298.
38. Dean Rusk, Secretary of State 1961–69.
39. Bhutto (1976), p. 21.
40. Gauhar (1993), pp. 352–3.
41. Khan (1997), pp. 182–84.
42. Kissinger (1979), p. 849.
43. Gromyko (1989), p. 247.

44. 'They developed a conspiratorial approach to foreign policy management. They tried not to let anyone else have a full picture, even if it meant deceiving them.' Lawrence Eagleburger, quoted in Isaacson (1993), p. 209.
45. Isaacson (1993), pp. 406–7.
46. Recalled in Kissinger (1979), p. 847.
47. *Memorandum of Conversation No. 4,* 24 February 1972, p. 28 (National Security Archive, Washington). The rest of Nixon's obviously disparaging remarks against the subcontinentals have been blacked over and marked 'Sanitizied'. Kissinger, however, gives the game away by adding gratuitously: 'The President meant the American Indians.'
48. Isaacson (1993), p. 148.

1

CONTACT

The first formal contact initiated by President Nixon, it will be recalled, occurred during his meeting with President Yahya Khan in August 1969 at Lahore, Pakistan. The first document in Yahya Khan's file is a message three months later, dated 10 October 1969, sent to President Yahya Khan by Major-General Sher Ali Khan Pataudi, then his Minister for Information and Broadcasting.[1] The message, in cypher, came through the Pakistan Embassy in Washington and was marked 'Top Secret. Personal for President's eyes (eyes) only':

Met Kissinger just now. Conveyed your message for President Nixon. Discussed your approach to the problem. He agreed that to be effective it must be kept at highest level. Asked him for specific points for discussion from United States point of view. He said that he would have to think over this and would let us have them through Hilaly in a few days. In the meantime to help atmosphere and to assist us in our task, even if it would be a very small measure, we may convey to Chinese that the two destroyers in straits of Formosa that have been irksome to them (the Chinese) are being withdrawn. But this gesture does not affect United States position regarding Formosa or anything else at this stage. He requested that this be restricted to the most confidential level. And suggested that you may kindly send for Chinese

Ambassador [Zhang Tong[2]] and convey this to him yourself with no one else there.

I have been meeting officials here—most interesting and I hope beneficial for us. More when we meet Insha Allah.

After receiving it on 13 October and reading it, President Yahya Khan marked it to his Military Secretary with the instruction: 'P.U. [Put up] when Gen. Sher Ali returns.'

Five days later, on 15 October 1969, Ambassador Agha Hilaly wrote in longhand to President Yahya Khan:

My dear Sir,

I wonder if we have made any progress in talking to the Chinese about President Nixon's desire to bring about a thaw in Sino-American relations? I did not write to the Foreign Office as I knew that at President Nixon's request you had agreed not to deal with this issue through the State Department & our own Foreign Office.

When Gen Sher Ali Khan came here & told me that you wanted him to see Kissinger about this matter, I asked him whether he had any progress to report. He replied that you had not been able to take up the matter with the Chinese yet as you wanted to hold discussions at the highest level only— & this was not possible unless you went to China or Chou En Lai came to Pakistan. Gen Sher also told me that before you contacted the Chinese you would like to know from the Americans the specific points which the U.S. would like you to take up with them.

I accordingly took Gen Sher Ali to Kissinger & the General's cypher telegram to you No. 543 dated 10 October explains what happened at that interview. I enclose a supplementary note about it which I prepared for my own record at the time.[3] You can see from it that the White House continues to be anxious to make some progress in breaking the U.S.-China deadlock. I do not know if the Americans are using any other channel[4] to contact Peking since we gave them to understand that we would prefer to wait for Chou En Lai's visit but the trend of Kissinger's talk with Gen Sher Ali & me showed that White House was still very interested in <u>our</u> doing something with the Chinese on its behalf.

You might have seen my cypher telegram to Foreign Secretary [Sultan M. Khan[5]] regarding today's Vietnam moratorium demonstrations in this country. The Nixon administration & Republican leaders are seriously disturbed about the amount of domestic pressure being put on them for a quick withdrawal from Vietnam. What began as an idle threat by a small radical section of the student community has snowballed into massive demonstrations by millions spread over all professions. Almost overnight it appears as if vast sections of the public have lost their trust in the Nixon administration & do not believe that it intends to implement its promise to terminate American involvement in the Vietnam war. The same credibility gap between the Administration & the public which led to the fall of Johnson has reappeared & is now confronting the Nixon Govt. The Administration is reported to be almost desperately looking for help from third countries which can mediate between it & and the North Vietnamese & thus give a prod to the Paris negotiations. I understand that the French Govt. are playing a prominent part in this matter.

At a time like this anything we can do to help Nixon is likely to prove beneficial to us. We have no representation at Hanoi & no leverage with the North Vietnamese. We can therefore do nothing to help the Americans in their present dilemma in Vietnam. This seems, however, to be a psychological moment to offer them our friendly services at least in regard to their beginning a dialogue with China. I assume of course that our relations with the Chinese are strong enough to allow us to talk in frankness & secrecy with the Chinese.

I wonder if you sent any message to top Chinese leaders through Gen Abdul Hamid Khan on his recent visit to China?[6]

If so the Chinese reaction obtained by him may be conveyed by us to Kissinger quickly. I would be grateful if you could let me know as Kissinger has already asked us (vide my enclosed note) whether we utilised the General's visit for this purpose.

Also, may I tell Kissinger that his message to you regarding the withdrawal of two destroyers from the Straits of Formosa was passed to the Chinese Ambassador?

Yahya Khan read Hilaly's letter on 24 October and instructed his Military Secretary: 'Keep this.'

On 14 February 1970, Pakistan's Foreign Secretary Sultan M. Khan (as yet in the dark about communications flowing from his subordinate Hilaly in Washington and his superior President Yahya in Islamabad) sent a handwritten message to Ambassador Hilaly to be conveyed to Mr Kissinger. It read:

The initiatives taken by the United States in recent months have encouraged the Chinese. It also seems to be their assessment that at present there is no collusion between Russia and the United States against China. They would, however, be very sensitive to any conclusion that their willingness for a meaningful dialogue with the United States is a reflection of any weakness on their part or the outcome of their fears about Russia. In fact proceeding from such a basis might well jeopardise future negotiations. In any case, the Chinese response is likely to be in very measured and cautious steps but China appears inclined towards a meaningful dialogue with the U.S. concerning all matters that divide the two countries. It should be anticipated however that the negotiations will be hard and difficult and a lot may be said for purposes of record but given trust between China and the U.S. the problems between the two countries could be solved through peaceful negotiations. The possibility of an expansion of the Vietnam war is seen as having lessened while war between China and USA is now seen as a very remote possibility.

On 23 February 1970, Ambassador Agha Hilaly wrote in his own hand to President Yahya Khan from Washington. Marking his letter 'For President's Eyes only', he began:

Foreign Secretary Sultan M. Khan sent me the enclosed top secret message in his own handwriting (I typed it out myself for easy reading) and asked me to convey it to Kissinger as from you to President Nixon. I have done so and have informed Sultan as in enclosed reply [not available] of my letter to him of today's date. What Kissinger said in reply I am writing below only to you. I have tried to reproduce the exact language used by him:-

Begins. 'President Nixon was discussing this very matter with me (Kissinger) at Camp David last night. He very greatly appreciates President Yahya's role in this matter & wishes to thank him very warmly. President Nixon would be grateful if President Yahya would tell the Chinese that the White House is as usual quite unable to control speculation in the American press about the Warsaw talks[7] but the White House will scrupulously avoid making any such statement that the present dialogue between the U.S. & China is due to the Chinese fear of Russia. The difficulty is that when such negotiations are carried on through formal diplomatic channels as in Warsaw it is not easy for the White House to maintain total discretion & silence because too many people see what is happening there. President Nixon would therefore be prepared to open a direct White House channel to Peking, if Peking would agree. The existence of such a channel would not be known outside the White House and we can guarantee total discretion.' Ends.[8]

After giving this message for transmission to you, Kissinger especially asked me not to send a code telegram about it but write it out in my own hand for your eyes only. (Perhaps you will be calling the Chinese Ambassador to give this message to him yourself?)

I trust you are keeping very fit & well in spite of your great pre-occupations. Kindly let me know as soon as Chou En Lai's date for visiting you is fixed. The White House keeps on enquiring from me.

Hilaly concluded on a personal note: 'I hope to come to Pakistan on my once in three year's home leave some time after June'.

Ambassador Agha Hilaly wrote again to President Yahya Khan on 26 March 1970:

Agha Shahi,[9] who has just returned from Pakistan, told me that you wanted him to tell me that you "were giving consideration" to the matter I had referred to in my "handwritten letter". I presume you were referring to my letter of 23rd Feb in which I sent you the message Kissinger wanted to be conveyed to Chou En Lai—that the White House was prepared to open a direct secret channel to Peking if the Chinese also agreed.

Kissinger will probably send for me soon to ask me whether we have transmitted that message to Peking. I do not know whether you found time to send for the Chinese Ambassador to do so or preferred to do it in some other way. Recently you met Kuo Mo Jo [Kang Mao Zhao].[10] I am sure you will let me have something for the information of Kissinger & President Nixon in regard to their message, even if it is only to say that we have conveyed it to Chou En Lai & are awaiting his reaction.

Vice Premier Kang Mao Zhao was one of a number of visitors to Pakistan during this period. The others included

King Hussein of Jordan and his younger brother Crown Prince Hassan. Parallel to playing host to foreign dignitaries, Yahya Khan was involved domestically with the declaration of general elections in the country. He announced and then promulgated the Legal Framework Order to regulate the conduct of the elections, and to explain its mechanism he met the editors of Pakistani journals and newspapers as well as foreign correspondents on an ominous date—1 April 1970.

In Ambassador Hilaly's next letter to President Yahya, written five days later on 6 April 1970, Hilaly recounted the efforts he was making on his side of the Atlantic to contain the damage caused to Pakistan's image in US newspaper circles. He reported that he had been complaining repeatedly to the management of the *New York Times* that they had been printing 'rather critical and adverse reports' about Pakistan. To counter an unfavourable piece by Chester Bowles, Hilaly arranged for a rejoinder to be published by Benjamin H. Oehlert, Jr., a former US Ambassador to Pakistan. 'Perhaps as a result of my repeated pressure they [the *New York Times*] sent their correspondent Sydney Schanberg to Pakistan recently'. Hilaly enclosed a copy of his 'favourable despatch' dated 1 April, which appeared in the issue of 6 April 1970.

The East Pakistan crisis remained at the forefront of everyone's consciousness for differing reasons, including President Nixon's. When Ambassador Hilaly met him on 14 May along with other delegates to the CENTO conference, he asked pointed questions of the beleaguered Ambassador. Hilaly's replies, if not entirely plausible, were at least innovative. In the short Note prepared by Hilaly on the discussion held on 14 May 1970 between President Nixon and his team at the White House and the heads of the Iranian, British, Turkish and Pakistani delegations to the CENTO meeting, Hilaly drew Yahya Khan's attention to his advocacy before President Nixon against the 'massive Indian build up', which he contended 'upset Pakistan's military balance with India.' Hilaly presented the following argument to Nixon:

A regional alliance pre-supposed that the partners had common interests. Therefore, a threat to one from <u>any</u> direction should be considered as a common threat by the others. The strengthening of each member was in the common interest of the others. It was therefore imperative for Pakistan to be helped to strengthen its defensive potential. In this connection he pointed out that the 1965 ban on the sale of American arms to Pakistan had still not been removed. He emphasised that it is not in the interest of the partners that Pakistan should be forced to become completely dependent for her military hardware on the Soviet Union or China.

President Nixon responded by referring to 'the days of the Eisenhower Administration when Pakistan enjoyed a special relationship with the US'. He said with the passage of time the situation had changed. This problem of arms was a very difficult problem. However, to quote the President 'we are giving much consideration to it'. Nixon then asked Hilaly about the situation in East Pakistan. Hilaly replied 'that the political situation was normal and electioneering was going on in full force, as was the case in West Pakistan.' In reply to another question by Nixon about the food situation in East Pakistan, Hilaly responded with the observation that, 'West Pakistan was self-sufficient in wheat and surplus in rice but there was a rice deficit in East Pakistan, which it would take some time to overcome.' Hilaly added gratuitously, with more optimism than accuracy, 'However the people of East Pakistan were not as completely dependent on rice as they once were. They were interchanging wheat with rice in their daily diet.'

In the concluding paragraph of his letter to President Yahya, Hilaly added the snippet that both White House and State Department officials had told his deputy, Minister Farooqi,[11] that 'your Ambassador's advocacy at the White House meeting has made an impact on President Nixon.'

In the context of Pakistan's need for the supply of arms whether from the US or the Chinese, the subsequent conversation between Premier Zhou Enlai and President Nixon during their meeting in Beijing on 23 February 1972 is of especial interest:

> *Premier Chou En-lai*: Of course we don't want to interfere in other's internal affairs, but Yahya really did not lead his troops in East Pakistan well. Even though we assisted with armaments, we didn't send a single military personnel, what the Soviet Union calls military adviser. We only sent some people to train in the use of the planes and guns we sent, and afterwards brought those people back.

After some intervening discussion, Nixon returned to this subject with the following admission:

> *President Nixon*: We have a problem with regard to military assistance, because of our Congress, and as I informed the Prime Minister and as the Deputy Foreign Minister [Qiao Guan Hua[12]] knows, American public opinion opposes military assistance to Pakistan. Incidentally, in retrospect it is my belief that had we been able to provide more assistance to Pakistan it would have averted war, because India would not have been tempted to win what they thought was a cheap victory. But that is water over the dam.[13]

Reverting though to events before the 1971 war, Hilaly wrote to Yahya Khan on 11 August 1970 from Palm Beach, Florida, en route to Mexico City.[14] He expressed happiness on hearing from his brother Agha Shahi, that 'there is a reasonable chance of your visiting the U.N. in New York in the third week of October.' Hilaly added that the 'White House is very exercised at the prospect of over 50 heads of State and heads of Government arriving simultaneously in this country, for addressing the General Assembly. In all probability, President Nixon will himself move over to New York to meet them, and give them a mass banquet. That, the White House people feel, will absolve him of any further official responsibility for their visits and it will probably be left to them to visit Washington entirely privately, if they wish to do so. Nothing is settled yet but I am watching developments.'

On 4 September 1970, Ambassador Agha Hilaly wrote again to President Yahya Khan, this time to report that 'our Government on the whole is now presenting a favourable picture both to its own nationals here as well as to Americans.' Referring to his earlier news about the congregation of heads of state at the forthcoming UN General Assembly, Hilaly enthused:

> I am absolutely delighted to hear from Agha Shahi that you are accepting U. Thant's[15] invitation to address the U.N. General Assembly in October. The picture of Pakistan, which had become so shaky and blurred abroad, having improved so much in the last one year, the time is now certainly ripe for the President of Pakistan to appear before the premier international and world organization to project his image in person.

Hilaly concluded on a note of self-projection:

> Hearing that you will be paying a State visit to Nepal on the 27th of this month, I wrote to Foreign Secretary that I will be in Pakistan on short leave for private affairs at that time and if he had no objection could he take your orders as to whether you would like to include me in your entourage for that visit because (a) I would like very much to see the magnificent tiger hunt the King of Nepal would be organizing in your honour (such occasions are almost historical and rare even in Nepal) and (b) the King and his Ministers have a special regard for me because of the very important help I organized for them when I was accredited to Nepal in 1961–63 (arranged PIA service, international news despatches, communications facility for their airport, training of Nepalies as pilots for the Nepal Airlines etc.) I assured the Foreign Secretary also that it is certainly not unusual for Ambassadors from other countries to be included in the Head of State's entourage on such visits on personal grounds.

Sensing that the Foreign Secretary may have preferred him at such a critical juncture to be in the front seat in Washington rather than in the back of an elephant's howdah in the jungles of Nepal, Hilaly ended his letter: 'As I have not heard from him in reply, apparently my request was not found acceptable.'[16]

The dramatic news of the supply of American weapons to Pakistan was the subject of Ambassador Hilaly's next letter to President Yahya Khan, a month later on 8 October 1970. Quoting the scoop by a prominent political commentator Warren Unna on WETA/TV news panel programme on 6 October, Hilaly informed his President:

> He [Unna] said that President Nixon took a personal decision to let us have some bombers, fighters and armoured personnel carriers at 'marked down rates applicable to military surplus

stores.' As you will see from the enclosed gist of his remarks supplied to us by the State Department today [see Appendix B] he specially mentioned that in taking this personal decision, President Nixon was 'heavily persuaded' by me.

In a second paragraph, Hilaly added:

I am glad to report that the White House is very appreciative of the fact that we kept the news secret for over three months until the fate of the Cooper-Church amendment was decided in Congress and until President Nixon was able to lift the ban on the sale of arms to Greece. I believe General Collins in Islamabad had already started discussion regarding terms and quantities with Ghias ud-Din Ahmad.[17]

Hilaly concluded:

I am delighted that you have reconsidered the question of visiting this country for the U.N. anniversary and will be arriving here soon. I am in touch with my brother in New York about your programme there and am awaiting President Nixon's decision about the date of his meeting with you to prepare your Washington programme.

President Yahya flew to New York, arriving there on 20 October. On the following day, 21 October, he addressed the Commemorative Session of the United Nations, met the editors of *Time* and *Life* magazines in the afternoon, and in the evening had dinner with President Ceaucescu of Romania. It is not reported whether they compared notes on President Nixon's use of both of them as 'secret channels' to China. From New York Yahya Khan went to Washington for a meeting with President Nixon at the White House on 25 October. Nixon included the following recollection of Yahya's visit in his memoirs:

On 25 October President Yahya Khan of Pakistan came to see me, and I used the occasion to establish the 'Yahya channel'. We had discussed the idea in general terms when I saw him on my visit to Pakistan in July 1969. Now I told him that we had decided to try to normalise our relations with China, I asked for his help as an intermediary.

"Of course we will do anything we can to help," Yahya said, "but you must know how difficult this will be. Old enemies do not exactly become new friends. It will be slow, and you must be prepared for setbacks."[18]

The newspaper reports of Yahya Khan's visit mention that 'President Nixon also showed considerable interest in President Yahya Khan's recent visit to Moscow[19] and his coming visit to Peking on November 10. The two Presidents were joined by their advisers after they conferred privately.' A specific mention is made of Kissinger's participation: 'President Nixon's Foreign Affairs Assistant Henry Kissinger was present for some time during the Nixon-Yahya talks, which were held in a cordial atmosphere.'[20]

En route home, President Yahya stopped over in Paris on 26 October to confer with French President Georges Pompidou, Meanwhile, Ambassador Hilaly scanned the American newspapers for coverage of Yahya's visit to Washington, and on 27 October sent some clippings to the President, with a note: 'You may like to see the enclosed front page coverage given the day after you left (Monday, October 26) by the *Washington Post* to your meeting with President Nixon.' Hilaly assured Yahya Khan of the special status he enjoyed in the White House by mentioning: 'Of the seven Heads of States and Chiefs of Government who met President Nixon, including Emperor of Ethiopia [Haile Selassie I], the *Washington Post* published only your picture with President Nixon.'[21]

Yahya Khan reached Rawalpindi on 28 October 1970, on the same day as the Awami League leader Sheikh Mujibur Rahman announced his explosive (and ultimately secessionist) Six Point Plan. Yahya Khan flew to China from Dacca on 9 November to meet Premier Zhou Enlai. The *Dawn* carried a bland report: 'Though there is no formal agenda for the talks, indications available in informed quarters here (Dacca) have raised substantial hopes for much greater collaboration between the two countries in various spheres, especially in the economic field.'

Yahya Khan stayed in China for five days, from 10 to 15 November 1970. His reception on arrival, according to Foreign Secretary Sultan M. Khan, who had witnessed many before and many since, was 'the most elaborate, colourful and magnificent given to any visiting Head of State in China.' Yahya Khan was welcomed personally by Premier Zhou Enlai. Later, on 12 November, President Yahya Khan and Premier Zhou Enlai conferred without aides in the privacy of the guesthouse where Yahya had been accommodated. (It was formerly the French Embassy and later the residence in exile of Prince Norodom Sihanouk of Cambodia.) According to a report in *Dawn*: 'They also discussed plans for further cooperation between Pakistan and China.' In fact, during this session Yahya conveyed Nixon's proposals for a meeting.

The Foreign Secretary however felt some pique at being excluded from these discussions and expressed his disappointment later: 'Yahya Khan was the lone participant from the Pakistan side and none of us who were with him in Peking knew about the Nixon proposal. For better or worse, he had taken on this onerous responsibility without the benefit of consultation and discussion with any of his advisers.'[22]

Premier Zhou Enlai left no mountain unturned to demonstrate support for Yahya Khan both officially by the Chinese government and personally by himself. Economic loans given by China were ceremoniously written off and agreements for military equipment were signed in the Great Hall of the People. At the dinner given by the Pakistan ambassador Mr K.M. Kaiser,[23] Premier Zhou Enlai made an unexpected and, for the Chinese leadership, unprecedented announcement. In reply to an invitation by Yahya Khan to visit Pakistan, Zhou Enlai responded by announcing that he would visit Pakistan *after* the December 1970 elections, 'when Yahya would have been elected President.' Understandably after such an unequivocal endorsement, Yahya Khan returned from his visit as 'happy and relaxed' as he had been throughout his visit.[24]

Now Yahya Khan had decided to include the Foreign Secretary Sultan M. Khan in the plot. Sultan Khan[25] had served first as deputy Chief at the Pakistan Embassy in Beijing in the 1950s and later as Ambassador to China (1966–1968). Sultan M. Khan recalled:

On 22nd November, 1970, after I had discussed some foreign policy papers with Yahya Khan, he said that there was an important and extremely sensitive task which he wished to entrust to me and that only he and I were to handle it in future. He then gave an account of his talks with Nixon in Washington in October and his subsequent talks in Beijing with Chou En-lai. Yahya Khan added that the channel of communication to Dr. Kissinger would be Mr. Hilaly, the Pakistani Ambassador in Washington, and to Chou En-lai, the Chinese Ambassador [Zhang Tong] in Islamabad. Stressing the need for secrecy, he said that all messages should be hand-written to eliminate the risk of leakage through secretaries and this routine was followed until the conclusion of the visit.[26]

On the following day, 23 November 1970, President
Yahya took down a secret message from the Chinese. This
was written in longhand by the Foreign Secretary Sultan
M. Khan, and sent to Ambassador Agha Hilaly in
Washington:

My dear Hilaly,

During the meeting at Washington on 25 October, our
President was requested by President Nixon to convey to
Chinese leaders his desire for establishing direct, secret
contacts, at whatever level they considered appropriate, so
that serious discussions could take place without the blaze of
publicity.

    This was duly conveyed and Premier Chou En Lai's reply,
given after three days of deliberation, is as follows:-

'This (meaning, the reply) is not from me alone but from
Chairman Mao and [Lin Piao / crossed out] Vice Chairman
Lin Piao as well.

'We thank the President of Pakistan for conveying to us orally
a message from President Nixon.

'China has always been willing and has always tried to
negotiate by peaceful means.

'Taiwan and the Straits of Taiwan are an [integral / crossed
out] unalienable part of China, which have now been occupied
by foreign troops of United States for the last fifteen years.
Negotiations and talks have been going on with no results
whatsoever.

'In order to discuss the subject of vacation of China's
territory, called Taiwan, a special envoy from President Nixon
will be most welcome in Peking.'

When the matter was first broached with Premier Chou En Lai he observed that:-

'We have had messages from the United States from different sources in the past, but this is the first time that a proposal has come from a Head (of State / Govt.) through a Head, to a Head! The United States knows that Pakistan is a great friend of China and therefore we attach great importance to it (message).'

You may add that it is significant that Premier Chou En Lai did not accept or reject the proposal as soon as it was made, and that he consulted Mao and Lin Piao before giving the answer. This, in itself, in the President's view, reflects a trend which holds out some possibilities. Further, at no stage during the discussions with the Chinese leaders did they indulge in vehement criticism of the United States. The banquet speech of Vice-Chairman Tung Pi Wu also made no references to United States by name. These are additional indications of moderation in Chinese approach to their relations with the United States.

Kindly convey the foregoing to Dr. Kissinger <u>orally</u>. You may in the interest of preciseness read out this letter to him, and thereafter destroy it. No notes or copy of this should be retained either in your office. Kindly confirm receipt and destruction after necessary action.

This message from its very language was clearly of historic significance. It remained undespatched, however, somewhere between the Presidency and the Foreign Office, even though the letter is clearly marked with the date '23/11/70', a Foreign Office despatch reference 'FS/U-C/1970', and the notation 'By Bag'. The explanation by Foreign Secretary Sultan M. Khan for the delay in transmission was published only recently: 'It is, in fact, possible to explain the delays which this vital information suffered. Firstly, it was delayed because Yahya Khan, on his return from Beijing, was distracted by the cyclone devastation in East Pakistan and the launching of the national elections, and secondly, because when my own message of 23 November reached Washington two days later, our Ambassador [Hilaly] was away in Mexico, where he was concurrently Ambassador. And so it was not until 9 December that the information reached Nixon.'[27]

However anxious Kissinger may have been in Washington, his concern could not be compared to the natural and man-made disasters which beset Yahya Khan during the twenty days following his return from Peking. On 24 November 1970 Yahya flew to Dacca to supervise relief work after a cyclone had hit East Pakistan. He returned to Rawalpindi on 3 December, was in Peshawar two days later, and came back to Rawalpindi in time to vote during the general elections held within the ambit of his Legal Framework Order promulgated on 30 March 1970.

On the morning of 8 December, Yahya learned, as did the equally surprised political contestants that, even according to the unconfirmed results, Sheikh Mujibur Rahman's Awami League had swept the polls in East Pakistan, winning 151 out of 153 seats in the Provincial Assembly, while in West Pakistan Zulfikar Ali Bhutto's Pakistan People's Party (PPP) had contradicted predictions, unsettled a number of feudals, and won 68 out of 82 seats in the Punjab alone. Sindh, being his home province, Bhutto regarded as safely in the bag anyway.[28]

In Washington, Dr Kissinger, waiting for a response from the Chinese, became perplexed by the delay. He wrote afterwards: 'President Yahya was in China from November 10 to 15 and we assumed nothing had happened. Then three weeks later, on December 8, Ambassador Hilaly contacted Hal Saunders[29] of my staff and said he had "a message" for me relating to Yahya's trip. We never received an adequate explanation why Yahya waited nearly three weeks after his return to Pakistan to transmit the message. Perhaps the Chinese for their own reasons established a date after which it could be communicated; perhaps the reason was Yahya's careful precautions.'[30]

The following evening, on 9 December, Kissinger gave an appointment to Ambassador Hilaly. 'I invited Hilaly to the White House the next day, where in my office a few minutes after 6.00 p.m. he produced an envelope containing a hand-written missive on white, blue-lined paper which had been carried to him by hand, Yahya not trusting the security of cable communications.' Hilaly told Kissinger that he was not authorised to leave Yahya's message with him. 'He therefore had to dictate it, speaking slowly as I copied it down.'[31]

Kissinger was too busy to feel any excitement. But he did recognise even at the time that the message being conveyed however belatedly, by Hilaly was 'an event of importance'. He interpreted it as the Chinese had intended him to—not 'as an indirect subtle signal to be disavowed at the first tremors of difficulty. It was an authoritative personal message to Richard Nixon from Chou En-lai, who emphasized that he spoke not only for himself but also for Chairman Mao and Vice Chairman Lin Piao [.] In short, a personal representative of the President was being invited to Peking.'[32]

President Nixon recalled the same memorable occasion in his *Memoirs:* 'On Dec 9 Chou En-lai sent word through President Yahya that my representative would be welcome in Peking for a discussion of the question of Taiwan. Chou stressed that the message did not come from him alone but had been approved by Chairman Mao and by Lin Piao, still a powerful figure at that time. With characteristic subtlety, Chou concluded with a play on words. "We have had messages from the United States from different sources in the past," he said, "but this is the first time that a proposal has come from a Head, through a Head, to a Head." Through Pakistani Ambassador Agha Hilaly we replied any meeting should not be limited to a discussion of Taiwan, and we proposed that Chinese and American representatives meet in Pakistan to discuss the possibility of a high-level meeting in Peking in the future.'[33]

Sultan M. Khan, the Foreign Secretary, in his published recollection of this event says: 'In the first message sent to Dr. Kissinger on Yahya Khan's behalf, in a diplomatic pouch,[34] Ambassador Hilaly was asked to read out its contents to Dr. Kissinger and not to hand over the communication itself. Yahya Khan added his own footnote to Chou En-lai's reply and said that although the proposed agenda appeared to limit the scope of the talks, this should not be interpreted literally. He felt certain that once direct contacts had been established, *everything* of interest to the two sides could be discussed. In any case, he pointed out, the issues involved were of such complexity that the initial meetings could only be used for defining the general principles of future discussions.

Dr. Kissinger's reaction on receiving the message was of tremendous relief. Like Zhou Enlai, Nixon, too, had a great deal at stake in taking this initiative and a Chinese rejection would have been a big set-back for him.'[35]

Contact having been established between the United States and China at the highest level, the next step was to identify who should perfect that contact. It was left to President Nixon to select his nominee.

NOTES

1. Sher Ali Khan Pataudi had served Yahya Khan's predecessor Ayub Khan as Chief of General Staff before being removed. He was Yahya Khan's opinionated and often controversial Minister for Information and Broadcasting from August 1969 until December 1970. 'Rumour was strong that he had in fact been dismissed, and it seems probable that Yahya Khan felt himself ill-served by him. But if Yahya Khan had been relying on the advice of Sher Ali Khan, that perhaps was unwise, for Sher Ali Khan was not trained in politics and his views were certainly not free of bias in some respects.' Feldman (1976), p. 97.
2. Zhang Tong, Chinese Ambassador to Pakistan (1969–74).
3. See Appendix A. The four-page note on Embassy of Pakistan letterhead was handwritten by Ambassador Hilaly.
4. Hilaly was apparently unaware of the Romanian channel being used by the US.
5. Sultan M. Khan began his career as an army officer in the British Indian Army and was briefly in the Indian Political Service before opting for the Pakistan Foreign Service in 1947. He had served as deputy chief at the Pakistan Embassy in Beijing in the 1950s and later as Ambassador to China (1966–1968), before becoming Foreign Secretary. He served as Ambassador to US (1972–73), and Ambassador to Japan (1974–76).
6. General Abdul Hamid Khan, COAS, visited China in October 1969.
7. Nixon's reference was to the periodical contacts between US and Chinese representatives at Warsaw, and in particular to the 135th such meeting on 20 January, 1970, at which US Ambassador Walter Stoessel announced to his counterpart Lei Yang (Charge d'Affaires, People's Republic of China) that 'the United States would be prepared to consider sending a representative to Peking for direct discussions with your officials or receiving a representative from your government in Washington for more thorough exploration of any of the subjects I have mentioned in my remarks today or other matters on which we might agree.' (Quoted in Kissinger [1979], p. 687.) Lei Yang had been instructed by Beijing to respond in a similar vein.

8. Summarized in Kissinger (1979), pp. 689–690. Kissinger adds: 'Nixon wrote "Good" on my memorandum reporting the conversation.'

9. Agha Shahi (brother of Ambassador Hilaly), Ambassador and Permanent Representative to the United Nations (1966–1972), Ambassador to China (1972–1973), Foreign Secretary (1973–1977), and Minister for Foreign Affairs (1977–1982).

10. Kang Mao Zhao, Vice Premier of the National Congress, PRC. He had arrived in Pakistan on a three day visit, between 10–12 March 1970. He met Yahya Khan on 11 March at Karachi. He retired as Vice Chairman of International Trade Promotion Commission.

11. Mr Z.M. Farooqi, Minister in Washington (1968–70), later Ambassador of Pakistan to Algiers (1972–73) and to Brazil (1978–79).

12. Later Vice Minister (1964–74) and Minister (1974–76). See Burr (1998), p. 499.

13. *Memorandum of Conversation No. 3,* 23 February 1972, pp. 7 and 9 (National Security Archive, Washington).

14. Agha Hilaly was also accredited Pakistan's Ambassador to Mexico.

15. U Thant, UN Secretary General, 1961–72.

16. President Yahya Khan paid an official visit to Nepal, arriving in Kathmandu on 27 September. During the visit the sudden death of President Nasser of Egypt was announced on 28 September, causing Yahya Khan to curtail his visit. The tiger hunt was cancelled.

17. Ghias ud-Din Ahmad, Secretary Defence, Government of Pakistan.

18. Nixon (1978), p. 546. Nixon met President Ceaucescu of Romania on the following day and discussed the Romanian channel with him.

19. Yahya Khan had visited Moscow in August 1970, reciprocating Premier Kosygin's earlier visit to Pakistan in the middle of 1969. Sultan Khan gives a vivid account of the clash of wills between Yahya Khan and his counterpart Podgorny when the latter 'insisted' that there should be a meeting between Yahya Khan and Mrs Indira Gandhi (Khan [1997], pp. 238–240).

20. *Dawn,* 27 October, 1970.

21. One of the unsuccessful contenders was Archbishop Makarios, President of Cyprus. A photograph of Yahya Khan and Nixon during this visit has been reproduced in Khan (1997), p. 461.

22. Khan (1997), p. 241.

23. Pakistan's Ambassador to the People's Republic of China (1970–73). He retired from Government service in September 1973.

24. Khan (1997), p. 243.

25. Sultan M. Khan belonged to the ruling family of the minor princely state of Jaora, near Bhopal in India. His courtly almost mandarin mien may explain why he empathized so closely with Premier Zhou Enlai (see Khan [1997], pp. 211–2).

26. Khan (1997), p. 247.

27. Khan (1997), p. 248.

28. The final results gave the PPP 81 out of 138 seats in the Punjab.

29. Harold (Hal) Saunders, Kissinger's senior staff assistant on the Middle East.

30. Kissinger (1979), p. 700.

31. Kissinger (1979), p. 700.

32. Kissinger (1979), p. 701.

33. Nixon (1978), pp. 546–7.

34. Sultan Khan does not say on which day the letter was actually despatched. He mentions in his *Memories & Reflections* that 'I do not definitely know what kept Yahya Khan from informing Nixon about the Chinese response for nearly two weeks after his return from Beijing' (Khan [1997], p. 246–7).

35. Khan (1997), pp. 247–8.

2

IGNITION

The response by the White House to Premier Zhou Enlai's historic message came within a week. Ambassador Hilaly was called by Dr Kissinger on the morning of 16 December 1970. Evidently Dr Kissinger was experiencing qualms about the level of secrecy maintainable within the Pakistan link in the communication chain. The inordinate delay in the transmission of Premier Zhou's 'Heads' message might have prompted Dr Kissinger's renewed emphasis on the need for utmost secrecy, even from the Foreign Office in Islamabad which contained a number of East Pakistanis on its staff.

Hilaly's hand-written message was captioned: 'Top Secret. Record of a discussion with Mr Henry Kissinger at the White House, Washington on 16th Dec. 1970.' It was accompanied by a typed, unsigned two page note:

I was asked by Mr Kissinger to come to the White House to see him at 11 AM this morning. He told me that in reply to the message sent by Premier Chou En Lai through President Yahya Khan (which I conveyed to him on 9th of December), President Nixon wished to send a fresh message to President Yahya Khan for passing it on to Premier Chou En Lai. He presumed this would be done through the Chinese Ambassador in Islamabad in the interest of top secrecy as the

White House wanted to restrict knowledge of these exchanges to as few individuals as possible. For example at the Washington end only President Nixon and he knew about this exchange of messages. Similarly, on our side he hoped only President Yahya would keep the exchange out of the purview. [*of our Foreign Office as that ... would ...in Pakistan as a result of the recent... balance ... of these top secret exchanges... any knowledge of the matter.* / Five sentences defaced by pen.]

I assured Mr Kissinger that I always communicated these messages direct to President Yahya by writing them out in my own hand and I was not sending copies of such letters [*through Foreign Office* / deleted]. Mr Kissinger then gave me a typed aide memoire in an open envelope, which was addressed to President Yahya Khan (enclosed). Before reading it, I asked him what it said. Mr Kissinger replied that in response to Premier Chou En Lai's suggestion that a Special Representative of President Nixon would be welcome in Peking to discuss the question of Taiwan, President Nixon wished to inform Premier Chou En Lai that the U.S. was prepared to attend a preliminary meeting at an early date at a location convenient to both sides, to discuss what arrangements should or could be made for sending a U.S. delegation to Peking for high level discussions.

In reply to a question from me Mr Kissinger said this preliminary meeting could take place in Rawalpindi if it would not embarrass President Yahya in any way. From the U.S. side, the representative might be retired Ambassador Robert Murphy[1] or Mr Dewey[2] or Ambassador David Bruce.[3] Or it could even be himself if the level of the Chinese representative warranted his making the journey. He could arrange to pay a visit to Saigon and under that cover arrange a halt in Pakistan to meet the Chinese representative.

Mr Kissinger added that if a U.S. delegation went to Peking thereafter, the discussions would not be restricted to the question of Taiwan but would embrace all matters connected with improving relations with the Chinese and reducing tensions.

In answer to another question from me, Mr Kissinger said it would not be difficult to comply with the Chinese request for withdrawing U.S. military forces from Taiwan. The only American military forces there at present were advisory and training missions.

The text of the unsigned typewritten note handed over by Dr Kissinger to Ambassador Hilaly read:

The U.S. representative at the meeting between the two sides in Warsaw on January 20, 1970, suggested that direct discussions be held either in Peking or Washington on the broad range of issues which lie between the People's Republic of China and the U.S., including the issue of Taiwan. This proposal was an outgrowth of the consistent policy of the United States Government to seek opportunities for negotiating the settlement of outstanding issues between the two governments. The United States therefore welcomed the remarks of the representative of the People's Republic of China at the Warsaw meeting of February 20, 1970, in expressing the willingness of the Government of the People's Republic of China to receive in Peking a U.S. representative of Ministerial rank or a special Presidential envoy.

In the light of the remarks of Premier Chou En Lai to President Yahya, as well as the continuing United States interest in U.S.-China discussions at a higher level, the United States Government believes it would be useful to begin discussions with a view of bringing about a higher-level meeting in Peking. The meeting in Peking would not be limited only to the Taiwan question but would encompass other steps designed to improve relations and reduce tensions. With respect to the U.S. military presence on Taiwan, however, the policy of the United States Government is to reduce its military presence in the region of East Asia and the Pacific as tensions in this region diminish.

The United States therefore proposes that representatives of the two Governments meet together at an early convenient moment in a location convenient to both sides to discuss the modalities of the higher-level meeting. These modalities would include the size of the delegations, the duration of the meeting, the agenda and a clear understanding on the status and amenities, which the U.S. delegation would enjoy while in the People's Republic of China.

Kissinger explained the sequence followed within the White House when drafting such carefully crafted responses: 'Our messages to the Chinese were first drafted by me by hand after discussion with the President. They then went generally through several additional drafts to take account of comments by Al Haig and Winston Lord and my own second thoughts. They were then typed and shown again to Nixon; my records show that he approved them without change.'[4] Such notes were typed on recycled Xerox paper without letterhead or watermark.[5]

The American reply sent by Kissinger on such plain paper was received by the Chinese in the first week of the New Year, on 5 January, 1971.[6]

For the next two months, no messages were forthcoming from the Chinese, at least none that the Americans could discern. In fact, the Chinese leadership was transmitting signals with such subtlety and finesse that they went undetected, even in the White House. The most significant of them was the sudden invitation in April 1971 extended in Nagoya (Japan) to an American team of Table Tennis athletes to visit China, and the special importance given to the team by officials during their stay there, including a meeting with Zhou Enlai himself. 'The Americans ...quickly invited the Chinese team to tour the United States. The invitation was accepted immediately,' wrote Kissinger. 'The whole enterprise was vintage Chou En-lai.

Like all Chinese moves, it had so many layers of meaning that the brilliantly painted surface was the least significant part.'[7]

Impatient with the silence from the Chinese side, it was agreed between Nixon and Kissinger to contact the Chinese directly. Kissinger recalled: 'Finally, on April 27 we decided to approach the Chinese directly. A courier was sent to Paris with a letter for Jean Sainteny, urgently requesting him to deliver to the Chinese Ambassador a formal proposal to open a channel with us in Paris. We chose Paris because of at least a possibility that the long Chinese silence in the Pakistan and Romanian channels might mean that neither was trusted. The letter, however, was never delivered. While it was still en route, the Pakistani channel became active at last and we stopped the letter.'[8]

Meanwhile, in Islamabad, the anxiously awaited message from China had already been delivered by the Chinese Ambassador to President Yahya Khan on 21 April 1970. The handwritten note on four sheets of paper printed 'President' was forwarded by Yahya Khan's Military Secretary on 24 April through the Foreign Office bag.

The text of the Chinese message was:

Premier Chou En Lai thanked President Yahya Khan for conveying the message of President Nixon on 5 Jan 71. Premier Chou En Lai is very grateful to President Yahya and he will be grateful if President Yahya conveys the following verbatim message to President Nixon.[9]

Owing to the situation at the time, it has not been possible to reply earlier to the message from the President of the USA to the Premier of the People's Republic of China.

At present contacts between the peoples of China & the United States are being reviewed. However, if the relations between China & the US are to be restored fundamentally, the US must withdraw all its Armed Forces from China's Taiwan and Taiwan Straits area. A solution to this crucial question can be found only through direct discussions between high-level responsible persons of the two countries. Therefore, the Chinese Govt. reaffirms its willingness to receive publically [*sic*] in Peking a special envoy of the President of the U.S. (for instance Mr Kissinger) or the US Secy. of State or even the President of the U.S. himself for a direct meeting and discussions. Of course, if the U.S. President considers that the time is not yet ripe, the matter may be deferred to a later date. As for the modalities, procedures and other details of the high-level meeting and discussions in Peking, as they are of no substantive significance, it is believed that it is entirely possible for proper arrangements to be made through the good offices of President Yahya Khan. April 21, 1971.[10]

Kissinger's recollections read:

The first indication came at 3.45 p.m. on April 27—word that Hilaly needed to see me urgently for five minutes. Told by Hal Saunders that I was leaving on vacation the next day, Hilaly insisted that his message could not wait. So I received him at 6.12 P.M. He handed me a handwritten two-page aide-memoire conveying a message from Chou En-lai in response to President Nixon's message of December 16 (received, we now learned, by the Chinese on January 5).

Kissinger asked Hilaly when this message had been received in Pakistan: 'After returning to his office, he called me to say that it had arrived on April 23. The delay was due to its having been sent to Washington by courier.' In fact, a note appended by the Military Secretary to the President to the original manuscript note states: 'Sent to Agha Hilali with President's letter (in own hand) on 24 Apr.' This is confirmed by Hilaly's cypher acknowledgment No. C-356 dated 28 April sent to the President through the Foreign Office and received on 29th:

> Top Secret. Strictly Personal and for President's eyes (eyes) only from Hilaly.

> Many thanks for your letter of April 24th. Delivered message yesterday. It was much appreciated and I was asked to convey grateful thanks and to say that a reply will be given in about a fortnight's time.

Hilaly left Kissinger's office, and almost immediately Kissinger went to see President Nixon to discuss the latest message. After ruminating over it, later that evening Nixon called Kissinger on the telephone and toyed with the names of possible emissaries. David Bruce? The ideal emissary, they both agreed, but perhaps not acceptable to the Chinese for being the head of the US team in Paris on the Vietnam talks. (Bruce was later to become Head of the first US Liaison Mission in Peking.) Other potential candidates were Nelson Rockefeller (Kissinger's mentor), George Bush, Elliott Richardson, and Tom Dewey (who had in fact died on 16 March 1971). A definite non-candidate was Secretary of State William Rogers who, although he enjoyed a special position of proximity to the President for being his personal friend,[11] suffered the more overpowering disability of heading the State Department which Nixon and Kissinger had assiduously kept out of the China connection.

Nixon waited until the next afternoon before informing Kissinger that he was to be the chosen emissary. Kissinger unravelled the complex reasons why Nixon would have chosen him: 'Only romantic outsiders believe that men who have prevailed in a hard struggle for power make decisions exclusively on the basis of analytical ideas.

Nixon's overriding motive was undoubtedly that I understood our policy best, and that being familiar with my complicated chief I would be able to arrange the sort of Peking visit for him with which Nixon would be most comfortable. He could ask me without embarrassment to raise the public relations requirements of his insistently eager advance men. Another factor was undoubtedly that of all the potential emissaries, I was the most subject to his control. I was on the White House staff; I had no means of publicizing my activities except through the White House press office; my success would be a Presidential success.'[12]

President Nixon's recollection, according to his memoirs, was that he and Kissinger 'spent the next few days' trying to decide who to send to Peking. Various names were discussed.

"Finally", I said, "Henry, I think you will have to do it."

He objected that, like Rogers, he had too much visibility.

I said, "I am confident that a man who can come and go undetected in Paris can get in and out of Peking before anyone finds out."[13]

To himself, and later to his readers, Kissinger admitted that whatever his complex motivations. Nixon had shown great courage. He had 'authorized a mission that, had it failed, would surely have produced a political catastrophe for him and an international catastrophe for his country.'[14]

Eager but cautious, both Nixon and Kissinger decided to make haste slowly: 'Having been kept waiting for four months, we did not wish to return a formal response immediately, lest we appear too eager [.] I called in Agha Hilaly on April 28 to give him an interim reply.'

Their reply was contained in a cypher telegram sent the same day by Ambassador Hilaly from the Pakistan Embassy in Washington to the Foreign Office, marked 'TOP SECRET. No circulation. For President's eyes only from Hilaly.' The text read:

1. Further to my previous telegram NC-356 of 28th April. Kissinger after discussing the matter with President Nixon sent for me again this afternoon and requested that following message be conveyed to President Yahya from President Nixon. Begins: 'I would like to send my very warm thanks for great and helpful role you have played in this matter. I particularly appreciate delicacy and tact with which you have handled these very important exchanges. Thereby you are making a personal contribution to international understanding and world peace. I would be grateful if you would thank Premier Chou En-lai for message he has sent me through you. I appreciate its constructive, positive and forthcoming nature. I will soon be sending a reply to it in the same spirit.' Ends.

2. Kissinger then said that President Nixon would be grateful if President Yahya when conveying above reply to Chou En-lai would give following advice to Chou En-lai as if it is President Yahya's personal (repeat personal) view and not (repeat not) as a direct request to Chinese from Nixon.

Begins. 'From my personal knowledge of Nixon and my Washington Ambassador's information, I feel that Nixon is very anxious to handle these negotiations for the next few weeks entirely by himself without allowing any American politician to interfere in them until a Government to Government channel could be established between Peking and Washington. My Ambassador in Washington thinks this is because President Nixon will find it harder to move quickly in the matter if American politicians are brought into picture and make an issue of it. I agree with this. It would appear therefore that it would be best if Chinese Govt. could avoid giving visas to any American politicians either Republicans or Democrats until President Nixon's reply has been received and White House designates an envoy to conduct these negotiations. Ambassador Hilaly was told clearly that President Nixon has no objection whatsoever to any other kind of American citizens being invited to visit China except politicians for the next few weeks. For example Chinese are free to invite any and every other category of American citizens like pressmen, artists, professors, sportsmen, etc., etc., if Chinese would like to do so as part of their people to people programme. Ambassador Hilaly was also told that President Nixon would not take more than two or three weeks to send a reply to Chou En-lai's message.' Ends.

3. I gathered impression from Kissinger that Nixon is very anxious that not only should you convey his formal reply in para 1 above to Premier Chou En-lai but also contents of para 2 above entirely as your (repeat your) views as he is reluctant to send this kind of advice direct to Chinese because it involves his saying that he does not want a certain kind of his fellow citizens to be permitted to visit China at present. He, therefore has specially requested that if you have no objection you may kindly oblige him by conveying the above advice as your own. I see no harm in our accepting Nixon's request and advising China. Nixon knows his political complications here better than ourselves or Chinese and as long as it suits national interest of China to cooperate with Nixon they should have no objection to doing so. So far as we are concerned we will be placing Nixon under an obligation to us at this particularly delicate moment in our national life when he is highest dignitary in this country insisting on pressure not (repeat not) being put on Yahya regime in regard to East Pakistan situation.

4. Kissinger has again emphasised to me that no one here except himself and Nixon are aware of this exchange of messages between White House and Peking and it is 'utmost' important that it should continue to remain as of utmost secrecy. Would be grateful if you could send me a signal that the above message has been transmitted to its destination.

In the margin, against Para 1 is scribbled 'Received on 30 April 71' and against Para 2 'Sent on 1 May 71'.

Hilaly received the confirmation he sought on 1 May. In a cypher message for the Ambassador from the President sent by his Military Secretary Major General Mohammad Ishaq, Hilaly was informed that 'President Nixon's message of thanks to Premier Chou En-lai through me conveyed to Chinese Ambassador this morning. Para 2 also conveyed as suggested.'

Mr Kissinger's apprehensions regarding the laxity of security arrangements in Pakistan were not entirely without foundation. On 1 May, one reads in the file an admonition from the Military Secretary to the President circulated to all officers concerned that:

Telegrams C-356 and C-360 from Parep Washington exclusively for the President, were put up to the President in the circulation folders—batch 238 and 240 respectively. These telegrams refer to a very sensitive subject and are in reply to the President's manuscript letter to the Ambassador. Their routine circulation is breach of security.

Unaware that the secrecy of his correspondence with the President was being compromised, Hilaly wrote to Yahya on 29 April, marking his letter 'Top Secret. No circulation. Strictly personal to President from Hilaly'. The letter read:

In my meetings with Kissinger both on 27th and 28th April I asked him to convey our warm thanks to President Nixon for having enforced restraint on State Department during the past six months when so many unfounded and unfriendly reports were being published in American press about our army action in East Pakistan and for withstanding pressure from press and Congress to express official sympathy on humanitarian grounds for rebels and to stop economic aid.

The reply Hilaly received was similar in tone to that of a tired mother's reaction in a argument amongst siblings—reassuring and at the same time mildly reproving:

Kissinger, in reply, told me that President Nixon would like me to inform President Yahya that owing to high regard he has for him and value he puts on his friendship, he had already ordered that administration should maintain an attitude of 'absolute correctness' towards East Pakistan affairs. President Nixon would continue to see to it that United States Government does nothing to embarrass President Yahya's Government. There were, of course, problems in American bureaucracy of which in my experience I should be aware. Nevertheless, if any pressure was exercised on me by administration President Nixon wants me to know that I could see Kissinger immediately with a view to President Nixon's attention being brought to it. President Nixon would intervene to put things right but of course White House should not be asked to intervene in each and every matter being discussed between us and State Department. Intervention from President Nixon should be to prevent any really decisive decision being taken against us.

So many people seemed to know of the secret exchanges and so many more who did not that any pronouncements, however innocuous about China, caused consternation at the White House. Even Chairman Mao was guilty (perhaps deliberately) of such a leak. Hilaly told President Yahya in his letter[15] No. C-363 of 2 May 1971:

Last night in nation wide television appearance President Nixon was asked whether Chairman Mao Tse Tung had invited him to visit Peking. This was because journalist Edgar Snow[16] who, it appears, is an old friend of Chairman Mao Tse Tung had visited Peking last December and had written an article in Life magazine stating that Chairman Mao Tse Tung said he would be happy to welcome Nixon in Peking whether he came as President or as a tourist. Secretary Rogers in television interview in London on April 28th had said in reply to a question that Chairman Mao Tse Tung's invitation could not have been meant seriously as it had been extended in such a casual way.[17]

Nixon seems to have instantly realised this kind of comment by Rogers could be misunderstood in Peking. (Secretary Rogers had already left for Paris before I conveyed Premier Chou En Lai's message to Kissinger on April 27th, and, therefore, Rogers could not have been aware that above invitation had been conveyed, formally also). I am sure that is why Nixon decided to avoid any such misunderstanding in Peking by dealing with this or any matter himself in his television interview last night. He neatly parried question put to him whether it was true that Mao Tse Tung had invited him. He said, 'I am not referring to any invitation. I am referring only to a hope and an expectation that at sometime in my life and in some capacity which, of course, does not put any deadline as to when I would do it, that I would hope going to mainland China.'

You might like mention this to Chinese Ambassador in Islamabad so that there is no misunderstanding about implications of Rogers' London statement. As I conveyed to you in my telegram No. C-360 dated April 28th, Kissinger after consulting Nixon about message I delivered to White House told me on 27th as well as April 28th that Nixon would be sending his considered reply to Chou En Lai's

message 'very soon'. Kissinger explained to me this meant in
two weeks time at the most. He also gave me to understand
that delay was due to the fact that he was leaving almost
immediately on his badly needed annual holiday implying
thereby that Nixon would not send reply without full and
detailed consultations with him.

Kissinger told me he would dearly love to go to Peking
himself, but there would be strong political reaction if he
undertook the mission personally. I did not ask him to
elaborate. Obviously he meant that there would be a howl not
only from Taiwan, but any sudden announcement like this
would provoke dangerous fear in Moscow, raise false hopes
within country and create panic in some of Asian countries
closely allied to United States.

Edgar Snow's revelation fomented further speculation
in the American press. An article by a journalist, Don
Irwin, appearing in the *Los Angeles Times* on 28 April and
in the *New York Post* the following day made Hilaly
suspect that Irwin's identification of President Yahya Khan
as 'the high-level channel' between Nixon and China could
have come only from the White House itself. This
suspicion was reinforced by the disclosure in the article
that President Yahya 'is said to have been advised of
Nixon's desire to improve relations with China when he
conferred in Washington with the U.S. President last
October 25th.'

Hilaly's handwritten letter of 4 May alludes to this:

You will be interested in seeing the two enclosed clippings
[of Irwin's articles] as they have referred to you. One is from
the New York Post & the other from the Los Angeles
Times—both dailies with very big circulation.

Edgar Snow, the famous writer who is stated to be an old
friend of Chairman Mao was the first to announce that while
in Peking last December, he had heard that messages were

being exchanged between Nixon & Chou En Lai through the help of a friendly third party. As soon as this news appeared in Life magazine there was intense speculation as to who could be the party carrying these messages. Up to now the guessing was confined to the Romanian Ambassador in Peking, the British Charge d'Affaires there and some French & Canadian diplomats. Now for the first time a correspondent by the name of Don Irwin has published a report (enclosed) that it was you. He must have obtained this information from the White House itself.

Whether this was a deliberate leak by the White House or not, it is having a good effect so far as we are concerned. Even if it was deliberately leaked, it could be due to a desire on the part of the White House to restrain important politicians & other leaders of public opinion here from pressing too hard on the Nixon administration for stopping economic aid and military sales to us. As I had been reporting to the Foreign Office, there is absolutely no doubt public pressure for such action by the Govt. has increased, is still increasing and could take on the proportions of the massive public campaign that was mounted here a couple of years ago supporting independence for Biafra.[18]

It is a matter of good fortune therefore that not only is President Nixon showing strong personal support for you and your Govt. at this juncture but also that we have obtained an opportunity to play such a big part in the relations between China and the U.S. when we so badly need Nixon's support to defeat the machinations of so many who have turned hostile to us over the East Pakistan affair.

In parentheses Hilaly reminded Yahya of the advice he had given earlier and which had remained unheeded:

I trust you remember what importance I attached to this particular role for you ever since you took charge of the country & President Nixon brought up the matter with you at Lahore on 31 July 1969 and the reluctance of Foreign

Secretary Yusuf & his officers to advise you to take up that
role.

Reverting to the China intermediacy, Hilaly concluded:

> Kissinger is returning to Washington by the end of this week
> & I will be seeing him on 10th or 11th May when I think we
> will be getting a further message for transmission to Peking.

During this time, Kissinger had been on vacation at Palm
Springs, where he spent his holiday preparing exhaustively
for his trip to China. 'I took with me...a bagful of books
on Chinese philosophy, history, and art. Winston Lord had
the responsibility for preparing the briefing materials, a
duty made excruciatingly painful by the necessity to keep
it secret from his beautiful, charming, and intelligent
Chinese-American wife, Betty,[19] born in Shanghai, whose
parents, originally from the Mainland, had close ties with
Taiwan. Winston set about to produce voluminous
notebooks on every subject that could conceivably come
up.'[20]

Separately Kissinger sent a message to Joseph Farland,
the US Ambassador to Pakistan, stationed in Islamabad,
asking him to fly to the US without telling his State
Department superiors 'on private business' but actually to
meet Kissinger at Palm Springs.[21] There, on 7 May,
Kissinger briefed him on the plans for his visit to China.
'At that point' Kissinger wrote, 'my idea was to meet
Chinese representatives either in Pakistan or at a
convenient airport in southern China.'

Farland's advice was that the meeting should be in China
rather than in Pakistan. If one's conversations were to be
overheard, Farland cautioned from experience, 'it would
be better to be taped by the Chinese, who would keep a
record anyway, than by the Pakistanis.' Kissinger agreed:

'I told Farland that I would set up a Navy back-channel via our naval attache in Karachi;[22] Admiral Elmo R. Zumwalt, Jr., the Chief of Naval Operations, had set up a similar channel for me with satisfactory results during the Berlin negotiations. (Later we found the Navy channel too cumbersome. With Helms's cooperation we worked out an effective system through the CIA.)'.[23]

Kissinger gave Farland an outline of his programme. He intended to make an information-gathering tour which would take him to Saigon, Bangkok, New Delhi, Islamabad, and Paris. 'Farland and I agreed that the most effective plan would be to have me arrive in Pakistan on a Friday morning. Farland would schedule a full day of activities both with the Embassy and with the Pakistani government. If President Yahya agreed, he might invite me to spend the weekend in some suitable retreat, say the Khyber Pass or some hill station. I would leave my plane at a conspicuous location at the airport. I would go to China in an American, Pakistani, or Chinese plane pre-positioned in Pakistan; we would make the final decision after we knew the venue and had looked into the feasibility. I would conspicuously reappear after an absence of no more than thirty-six hours and proceed westward to Paris. Farland thought all this was manageable; he promised to contact Yahya immediately upon his return. I told him that I would inform Hilaly of Farland's role.'[24]

Kissinger returned to Washington on 9 May with a draft reply to Zhou Enlai's message. He showed it to Nixon and after obtaining his approval he called Agha Hilaly to the White House at noon on 10 May. Returning to the Pakistan Embassy, Hilaly wrote the following five page message in longhand:

Kissinger sent for me this morning and gave me the enclosed note to be handed over by you to the Chinese Ambassador in Islamabad after you have read it. In doing this President Nixon would be most grateful if you could yourself advise the Chinese as follows (as if it is your opinion):-

1) It is most essential that Kissinger should meet Premier Chou En Lai or his high powered representative secretly first. It will serve the interests of both countries of expediting the Nixon-Chou En Lai personal discussions. No one except Kissinger is best qualified to have these discussions as he is the only person (repeat only) who knows President Nixon's thinking and his mind and can take decisions on the spot without having to refer back to Washington for advice & instructions.

2) Kissinger will make the trip to Vietnam for covering his visit to Pakistan. On way back he will drop in at Bangkok, Delhi and Islamabad as if for discussions about mutual problems. He will arrive Islamabad say on a Thursday. If he can be sent away by us on Saturday morning (or Friday night) secretly to China it will be best. He must return to Pindi by Sunday evening so that he can continue his return journey and reach—say Tehran—on Monday. He is ready to travel from Pindi airport to China & back either by a Pakistani plane or a Chinese plane but most essential feature of it should be secrecy. He will leave his Presidential jet at Pindi. We can announce that he has been taken away by us to see some place in North Pakistan for a weekend as a holiday. Which place he should announce as his holiday retreat for the weekend is left to us. (I suggested Hunza, Nathiagali, Kaghan, etc., etc.) He is open to our suggestions regarding this. If President Yahya would like to honour him by taking him personally to China, he and President Nixon will consider it a great privilege.[25] Otherwise of course Kissinger will travel to China with only one or two aides.

3) Kissinger's visit has to be kept a top secret as if Congress gets to hear abut it, Senate will want to hold an inquiry etc. as to why he had to go to China.

4) If Premier Chou En Lai would not like to meet him at a Chinese border town, he will gladly go to Peking but only in a safe jet plane—he would much prefer travelling in a Pakistani Boeing 707 for that long journey—not only on account of time & distance factor but also safety.

In great haste to catch today's bag.[26] Kindly wire to me that this letter reached you safely.

I am now taking M. M. Ahmad[27] to White House. The attitude there is very favourable & he will be wiring result to you by tomorrow.'

P.S. Kissinger wanted me also to inform you

1. That Farland was sent for secretly & told about this plan so as to keep him in picture. (He met Nixon in California 2/3 days ago). His embassy staff will not be told.

2. We should not use our own cypher for these messages as they have been compromised after East Pakistan affair.

The text of the message handed over by Kissinger to Hilaly was unsigned and typed on a plain unmarked sheet of paper. It read:

President Nixon has carefully studied the message of April 21, 1971, from Premier Chou En-Lai conveyed through the courtesy of President Yahya Khan. President Nixon agrees that direct high-level negotiations are necessary to resolve the issues dividing the United States of America and the People's Republic of China. Because of the importance he attaches to normalizing relations between our two countries, President Nixon is prepared to accept the suggestion of Premier Chou En-Lai that he visit Peking for direct conversations with the leaders of the People's Republic of China. At such a meeting each side would be free to raise the issue of principal concern to it.

In order to prepare the visit by President Nixon and to establish reliable contact with the leaders of the Chinese People's Republic, President Nixon proposes a preliminary <u>secret</u> meeting between his Assistant for National Security Affairs, Dr. Kissinger and Premier Chou En-Lai or another appropriate high-level Chinese official. Dr. Kissinger would be prepared to attend such a meeting on Chinese soil preferably at some location within flying distance from Pakistan to be suggested by the People's Republic of China. Dr. Kissinger would be authorized to discuss the circumstances which would make a visit by President Nixon most useful, the agenda of such a meeting, the time of such a visit and to begin a preliminary exchange of views on all subjects of mutual interest. If it should be thought desirable that a special emissary come to Peking publically [sic] between the secret visit to the People's Republic of China of Dr. Kissinger and the arrival of President Nixon, Dr. Kissinger will be authorized to arrange it. It is anticipated that the visit of President Nixon to Peking could be announced within a short time of the secret meeting between Dr. Kissinger and Premier Chou En-Lai. Dr. Kissinger will be prepared to come from June 15 onward.

It is proposed that the precise details of Dr. Kissinger's trip including location, duration of stay, communication and similar matters be discussed through the good offices of President Yahya Khan. <u>For secrecy, it is essential that no other channel be used. It is also understood that this first meeting between Dr. Kissinger and high officials of the People's Republic of China be strictly secret.</u> [28]

The handwritten notations on Hilaly's letter record that it was received by Yahya Khan on 17 May evening at Lahore and conveyed by him to the Chinese Ambassador two days later, on 19 May, at Karachi.

Converting Dr Kissinger's views into a facsimile of his own, President Yahya conveyed its contents to Ambassador Zhang Tong during their meeting at Karachi on 19 May 1971. The handwritten text, prepared for Yahya Khan to read out, was as follows:

Having conveyed the message verbatim from President Nixon to Your Excellency, I would like to give my impressions of the message.

Knowing President Nixon and Kissinger personally I would like to mention that Dr. Kissinger is the only person in the United States today who has the complete confidence of President Nixon, knows his mind fully, and is perhaps the most powerful adviser in the White House. It would be my sincere advice that Premier Chou En Lai himself meets Dr. Kissinger in this secret meeting. I believe that such a secret meeting with Dr. Kissinger on all matters on which he will be fully authorised by President Nixon to discuss and decide will be for the mutual benefit of both countries.

The suggestion of a secret meeting, I understand, is vital for President Nixon because of his desire to keep these discussions at his own level springs from an anxiety of anything going wrong in the discussions which will prove disastrous for the U.S.

In my earlier message to Your Excellency I had conveyed to you the desire of President Nixon to keep these negotiations secret from his politicians in his deep anxiety that these high level negotiations should not fail, and his personal desire to develop friendly relations with the People's Republic of

China. These factors explain his present request for a secret meeting.

I understand that Dr. Kissinger would fly to Vietnam; on his way back he would make stops at Bangkok, Delhi, and Islamabad. This is to act as a cover plan. From Islamabad he would like me to make him disappear to a holiday resort in North Pakistan. In actual fact he will be carried by P.I.A. to be delivered anywhere on Chinese soil, which you may like to suggest.

Due to the long flights via Ceylon to East Pakistan,[29] on to some place in China would amount to a waste of time. I would therefore suggest that perhaps the Northern Route into China will be time-saving. Since Dr. Kissinger will have to visit China, return to Islamabad and carry on his journey to Tehran and back home, the time available for the secret visit, including journey time will not be more than 2 to 3 days. I am suggesting these factors to Your Excellency which you may consider in deciding the place in China to be conveyed to me along with your reply to President Nixon's message. I understand also that Dr. Kissinger will be prepared even to visit Peking[30] if so desired by Your Excellency, keeping in mind the time factor.'

On 20 May 1971, Ambassador Hilaly sent a cypher message C-406 to President Yahya, marking it 'Absolutely restricted'. Decoded it read:

Kissinger again sending for me tomorrow with another important message for you to convey. He repeated that I should not transmit it to you telegraphically but send special Courier which of course I am reluctant to do in view of expenditure involved. I told him that he should consider sending it to Farland in Islamabad who could then come to Karachi to deliver it to you personally. Kissinger said he would take orders from above and let me know the final decision tomorrow. I have seen the message which is important but it is clearly aimed at making his proposed visit more possible. If he agrees to send it to you through Farland kindly agree to see Farland in Karachi before May 23 if Farland asks for such an interview.

The message delivered by Ambassador Farland by hand to President Yahya Khan on 22 May 1971 was, like its predecessors, typed and unsigned:

MESSAGE FOR THE GOVERNMENT OF THE PEOPLE'S REPUBLIC OF CHINA.

In case the People's Republic of China has not been apprised, the United States Government wishes to inform it of the following statement made by the President of the United States on May 20th, 1971: Quote The Governments of the United States and the Soviet Union, after reviewing the course of talks on the limitation of strategic armaments, have agreed to concentrate this year on working out an agreement for the limitation of the deployment of Anti-Ballistic Missile Systems (ABMs). They have also agreed that, together with concluding an agreement to limit all ABMs, they will agree on certain measures with respect to the limitation of Offensive Strategic Weapons. Quote The two sides are taking this course in the conviction that it will create favorable conditions for future negotiations to limit all strategic arms. These negotiations will be actively pursued. Unquote. President Nixon wishes to emphasize that it is his policy to conclude no agreement which could be directed against the People's Republic of China. Mr. Kissinger is prepared to include this issue and related questions on the agenda of the proposed meeting with the designated representative of the People's Republic of China.[31]

This message was conveyed to the Chinese Ambassador at 7 p.m. on the following day.

On 26 May 1971, Ambassador Agha Hilaly wrote again by hand to President Yahya Khan. His three page long letter read:

I received a telegram (No. 962 dated 18 May) from Karachi sent by your Mily. Secretary that my 'sealed letter had been received & delivered intact to the President.'

This did not make it clear to me that by that date the message to Premier Chou En Lai given to me by Kissinger on 10 May had been delivered to the Chinese Ambassador in Islamabad before you left for Karachi. When Kissinger asked me on 20th May whether it had been delivered, I replied in the affirmative as I was sure that since my letter must have reached you by 13th or 14th May, you must have sent for the Chinese Ambassador & passed it on to him before you left for Karachi. Evidently it is important for Kissinger to know the date by which these messages are given to the Chinese Ambassador in Islamabad.

As stated in my cypher telegram to you No. C 406 dated May 20, it was at my suggestion that Kissinger sent the next message to you (for transmission to the Chinese) through Farland. However when you get the reply from the Chinese Ambassador, I would be grateful if you would kindly send it to me by diplomatic bag for being delivered to Kissinger and not give it to Farland for doing so. As I have explained in my yesterday's telegram to you (No. C 430 dated 25 May), it is important for me to remain in this Chinese picture so that my requests about our own affairs are given full consideration. As a matter of fact Kissinger has no high opinion of Farland and told me frankly that he had to get him into the picture about this exchange of messages only as a precautionary measure and as a 'second string to the bow' in case I happened to be out of Washington at a particularly crucial moment. He therefore sent for Farland recently when President Nixon was in California (Kissinger was also with him there) and put him wise about these important exchanges so that he may know that he may be sometimes asked to carry such messages. Kissinger said he & President Nixon both much preferred to deal through me rather than through Farland. Hence my above request to you to send the Chinese replies to me by bag rather than give them to Farland.

Kissinger told me recently that he proposes to attend South Korea's President's installation on 1st July as a cover for his visit to Pakistan & Peking in which case he can arrive in Pakistan while on way to Seoul on June 20 or after the Seoul engagement reach Pakistan by evening of July 8. I trust you have given some thought to how we are going to arrange the two/three days disappearing trick for Kissinger after he reaches Rawalpindi.

The Foreign Secretary cyphered back to Ambassador Hilaly in Washington on 31 May 1971:

There is a very encouraging and positive response to the last message. Please convey that meeting will take place in the Capitol [*sic*] for which travel arrangements will be made by us. Level of meeting will be as proposed in your message.

Full message being transmitted by safe means, under separate intimation.[32]

President Nixon, in a speech at Alabama on 26 May to newspaper and television editors of thirteen Mid West states made a policy statement, during which he spoke of 'efforts to improve relations with Peking and help it to become a member of the world community.' He also hinted at the role China would play in a revised world order:

'Over the next 5 to ten years it (the USA) would have to share its leadership role with four other "centres of power"—Western Europe, Japan, the Soviet Union and the People's Republic of China,' and added for the benefit of those who look for such clues in policy statements: 'That is not a bad thing.'[33]

The 'very encouraging and positive' message referred to by Foreign Secretary Sultan Khan, containing Premier Zhou Enlai's response to Nixon's message, was delivered by the Chinese Ambassador to President Yahya Khan on 29 May 1971. The handwritten note on President's House notepaper recorded the following:

Premier Chou En Lai sincerely thanks His Excellency President Yahya Khan for most rapidly transmitting the three messages from President Nixon.

Premier Chou En Lai has seriously studied President Nixon's messages of April 29, May 17th and May 22nd 1971, and has reported with much pleasure to Chairman Mao Tse Tung that President Nixon is prepared to accept his suggestion to visit Peking for direct conversations with the leaders of the People's Republic of China. Chairman Mao Tse Tung has indicated that he welcomes President Nixon's visit and looks forward to that occasion when he may have direct conversations with His Excellency the President, in which each side would be free to raise the principal issue of concern to it. It goes without saying that the first question to be settled is the crucial issue between China and the United States which is the concrete way of the withdrawal of all U.S. Armed Forces from Taiwan & Taiwan Straits Area.

Premier Chou En Lai welcomes Dr. Kissinger to China as the U.S. representative who will come in advance for a preliminary secret meeting with high level Chinese officials to prepare and make necessary arrangements for President Nixon's visit to Peking.

Premier Chou En Lai suggests that it would be preferable for Dr. Kissinger to set a date between June 15th and 20th for his arrival in China, that Peking may be the location and that he may fly direct from Islamabad to a Peking[34] airport not open to the public. As for the flight, he may take a Pakistan Boeing aircraft, or a Chinese special plane can be sent to fly him to and from China, if needed. The talks plus the flight on both ways will probably take three or four days. If there is the desire to use his own telecommunication equipment on a temporary basis during his stay in Peking he may do so.

As it is difficult to keep Dr. Kissinger's trip strictly secret, he may well consider coming to the meeting in an open capacity. If secrecy is still desired, the Government of the People's Republic of China will on its part guarantee the strict maintenance of secrecy. When the talks have yielded results, the two sides may agree on a public announcement to be made after the meeting, if it is so desired.

As for other details, they may be discussed and arranged through President Yahya Khan directly with the Chinese Ambassador.

Premier Chou En Lai warmly looks forward to the meeting with Dr. Kissinger in Peking in the near future.[35]

To this communication, President Yahya dictated an addendum, transcribed in longhand by his Military Secretary:

I notice from the above message that the Premier has given an alternative for an open meeting between himself and Kissinger. Knowing Dr. Kissinger's desire to maintain strict secrecy which fact I have been impressing upon Premier Chou En Lai, the above message is indicative of the Premier's acceptance of the secret meeting for which he has given guarantee. The rest will depend upon US and Pakistan maintaining secrecy.

As regards arrangements on our part, I have discussed with the Chinese Ambassador and propose as follows:-

a. Dr. Kissinger arrives on a D Day.
b. After a 24 hour stop in Islamabad and a meal with me he will, ostensibly, make a trip to a place not open to public, in the Northern region. In actual fact, a Pakistani Boeing will carry him, along the Northern Route, direct to Peking from Islamabad. The time of the flight will be approximately seven hours.
c. On the completion of the mission, Dr. Kissinger will return to Islamabad to resume his onward journey.

If Dr. Kissinger would find it helpful, I am considering sending a high level Pakistani with him to Peking.

A covering note dated 31 May from the Military Secretary at Rawalpindi mentioned: 'The document, reproduced in my hand, was, as per President's direction, handed over to Foreign Secretary for despatch, through safest and quickest means to our Ambassador in Washington.' The 'safest and quickest way' was decided as being by courier.

In Washington, Kissinger had been alerted by Hilaly of the impending message. Kissinger wrote: 'On May 31 we received an excited but cryptic message from Hilaly: A long message from Peking was on its way by courier from Pakistan; Hilaly had been given only elliptical hints of its contents. Apparently it was encouraging; Hilaly was pretty sure that the Chinese accepted the essence of our proposal.'[36]

The Foreign Secretary Sultan M. Khan recalled in his memoirs that the 'proposed date for Kissinger's departure did not leave much time for sending messages in the normal way and it was decided to send Bashir Babar,[37] a Director from the Foreign Office, who looked after the North American desk, to Washington as a special courier with Premier Chou's message and to bring back a reply. Bashir Babar is a very calm and phlegmatic person and when I handed him the sealed envelope in the afternoon of 1st June, 1971 and asked him to depart that evening for Karachi, and from there take a flight that night for Washington DC, he expressed no surprise, or even curiosity about the purpose of his trip. As he was leaving with the sealed letter in hand, I told him to guard it with his life and in case he lost it, or the reply to it, he need not come back.![38] His only reaction was to smile and say "Yes sir".'[39]

Sultan Khan continued: 'In the meantime Dr. Kissinger had been alerted that a special courier was on the way with an important message. Bashir Babar arrived on the 2nd of June, and some measure of anxiety and sense of anticipation with which Kissinger awaited the message can be gauged by the fact that he noted the exact time (8.10 p.m. on 2nd June) that the message was handed over to him. The message was indeed of great historic significance and was the first substantive step in the re-establishment of direct contact between the U.S. and China after nearly twenty years.'[40]

Both Kissinger and Nixon remembered the arrival of this historic message, but have left differing accounts of the same moment. Kissinger recalled: 'I walked from my office in the West Wing over to the mansion to inform the President. Nixon was hosting a dinner for President Anastasio Somoza of Nicaragua. I told the military aide standing outside the State Dining Room that it was imperative for the President to see me for a few minutes as soon as he could. I paced the hall for several minutes, waiting. Around 9.30 the President came out. I told him about the message; buoyantly he took me to the Lincoln Sitting Room, found some brandy and two glasses, and proposed a toast to what had been and what remained to be done.'[41]

Nixon's memoirs give a significantly different account: 'After Pat and I had finished having coffee with our guests [the Somozas] in the Blue Room, I went to the Lincoln Sitting Room to do some paperwork and reading. In less than five minutes Kissinger walked in. He must have run most of way from the West Wing, because he was out of breath. He handed me two sheets of typewritten paper. "This just arrived in the Pakistani Embassy pouch," he said. "Hilaly rushed it over, and he was so excited when he gave it to me that his hands were shaking." Kissinger stood beaming as I read the message. [Nixon here reproduced an abridged text of the message.] "This is the most important communication that has come to an American President since the end of World War II," Kissinger said when I had finished reading.' Nixon opened a new bottle of Courvoisier brandy (a Christmas gift) and proposed a toast, the text of which finds common mention in both sets of memoirs: '"Henry, we are drinking a toast not to ourselves personally or to our success, or to our administration's policies which have made this message and tonight possible. Let us drink to generations to come who may have a better chance to live in peace because of what we have done".'[42]

NOTES

1. Robert D. Murphy (1894–1978). US Ambassador to Belgium, 1949.
2. Thomas E. Dewey (1902–1971), leading Republican and three-times Governor of New York (1943–55).
3. David Bruce (1898–1977), US Ambassador to France (1949–52), West Germany (1957–59) and Great Britain (1961–69).
4. Kissinger (1979), p. 718.
5. Kissinger (1979), p. 702.
6. Kissinger (1979), p. 714.
7. Kissinger (1979), p. 710.
8. Kissinger (1979), p. 713.
9. The handwritten notes in Yahya Khan's papers do not include the unusually formal preamble. The note begins: 'Thanks. Convey Chou message to Nixon. 5 January.'
10. Text reproduced in full in Kissinger (1979), p. 714.
11. See Isaacson (1992), p. 475.
12. Kissinger (1979), p. 717.
13. Nixon (1978), p. 550.
14. Kissinger (1979), p. 718.
15. The Foreign Office cypher clerk, keen perhaps to restrict the confidentiality of the correspondence even further, marked Hilaly's letter: 'For President's eye only.'
16. Edgar Snow (1905–72), author of *Red Star over China* (1937) and other significant books on China. He spent five months in 1936 with Mao Zedong and his revolutionaries in Baoan and the Yanan caves.
17. The article by Edgar Snow and Rogers' interview are referred to in Kissinger (1979), p. 720. Both Kissinger and Nixon were 'thunderstruck'.
18. A Reuter report of pressure by some Congressmen to stop military and economic assistance was enclosed.
19. This unqualified praise did not prevent her phone from being tapped by the White House. Taps were placed on 12 May 1970 and were kept there for the next nine months. See Isaacson (1992), p. 223.
20. Kissinger (1979), p. 721.
21. Kissinger felt that Farland could be trusted for being 'a man outside the regular Foreign Service Establishment. 'A

traditionalist,' Kissinger noted, 'would never have responded without reinsuring himself by a "personal" communication to his departmental chiefs in Washington.' Kissinger (1979), p. 722.

22. In both cases, Laird and naval chief Admiral Elmo R. Zumwalt, Jr. knew what was happening each step of the way, even if the CIA and State Department did not (Isaacson [1992], p. 201).

23. Kissinger (1979), p. 722.

24. Kissinger (1979), p. 723.

25. Yahya Khan recalled afterwards: 'He [Kissinger] was frightened about going to China and even had the audacity to ask me to accompany him. I told him that I'd send one of my generals along, if he wanted moral support, but I personally could not go. Chou En-lai had given me his word that he would look after him.' President Yahya Khan to author FSA, Rawalpindi, 2 August 1975.

26. Hilaly, in his haste, forgot to give a date to this letter.

27. M. M. Ahmad, then Economic Advisor to the President, and formerly Deputy Chairman, Planning Commission (1966–1970). Mr Ahmad suffered the indignity of being stabbed in the back while travelling in a lift in the Islamabad Secretariat. From the nature of the wound, it was confirmed by the police that the culprit was not in fact a government colleague.

28. Text has been reproduced in full also in Kissinger (1979), p. 724.

29. On 4 February 1971, the Indians put a ban on flights between West and East Pakistan over Indian territory.

30. The selection of place in China where Kissinger would meet his counterparts was less a matter of debate between the Chinese and the Americans than amongst Nixon and Kissinger, who remembered: 'He was eager to be known as the first American leader to visit Peking; he therefore requested me periodically to change the venue of my own visit to any other place in China. I did not know how to put this to either the Pakistanis or the Chinese.' (Kissinger [1979], p. 734.)

31. See Kissinger (1979), p. 725 for a reference to the breakthrough in the SALT negotiations which made this message a useful goodwill ploy.

32. No. O-3936 dated 31 May 1971, Foreign Islamabad to PAREP Washington.

33. Reported in *Dawn*, 26 May 1971.

34. Kissinger uses the word 'Chinese' instead of 'Peking' airport (see Kissinger [1979], p. 727).

35. Text reproduced in full in Kissinger (1979), pp. 726–7.
36. Kissinger (1979), p. 726.
37. Bashir Babar, later Pakistan's Ambassador to Lebanon (1980–84), High Commissioner to India (1989–90), and subsequently to Australia (1990–94).
38. For safekeeping, Mr Babar's wife sewed the letter in the pocket of his jacket.
39. Khan (1997), p. 251.
40. Khan (1997), p. 251.
41. Kissinger (1979), p. 727.
42. Nixon (1978), pp. 551–2, and Kissinger (1979), p. 727.

3

FLIGHT PLAN

President Nixon's reply to the 'most important communication' was rapid. Kissinger mentions: 'I handed our reply to Peking—composed by Winston Lord and me after many drafts—to Hilaly two days later in the afternoon of June 4.'[1]

The following day, on 5 June, Hilaly forwarded the two typewritten sheets to President Yahya, along with a supplementary Note prepared by him of his meeting with Kissinger the previous afternoon. In his covering letter, Hilaly wrote: 'Late yesterday evening Kissinger sent for me and gave me the enclosed typed message (original) for being passed on to the Chinese Ambassador for transmission to Peking.'

The text of the note itself reads:

President Nixon has carefully reviewed the May 29, 1971, message from Premier Chou en-Lai which President Yahya Khan so kindly conveyed. President Nixon looks forward with great pleasure to the opportunity of a personal meeting and discussions with the leaders of the People's Republic of China.

The President appreciates the warm welcome extended by Premier Chou en-Lai to his personal representative, Dr. Kissinger. Because of the shortness of time available and the need to arrange a suitable pretext for his travel, Dr. Kissinger now finds it impossible to leave Washington before the first week of July. Accordingly, President Nixon proposes that Dr. Kissinger arrive in China on July 9 and leave on July 11, flying in a Pakistani Boeing aircraft from Islamabad to Peking.

Dr. Kissinger will be authorized to discuss all issues of concern to both countries preliminary to President Nixon's visit to China, and to make all arrangements for the President's visit. Dr. Kissinger will not require his own telecommunication equipment. It is envisaged that four members of his personal staff will accompany him.

President Nixon appreciates the fact that the Government of the People's Republic of China will maintain strict secrecy with respect to Dr. Kissinger's visit and considers this essential. Dr. Kissinger will be authorized to settle on a possible communiqué to be issued sometime after his return to the United States if this is mutually desired.

Dr. Kissinger warmly looks forward to his visit to China and to his meeting with Premier Chou en-Lai. President Nixon considers this trip a very positive first step in improving relations between the United States and the People's Republic of China.[2]

Hilaly's letter continues with Kissinger's detailed messages to his future hosts:

2. He would be grateful if you also explain to the Chinese authorities that as secrecy was of the utmost importance, it would not be possible for him to ensure it if he announced any quick date for his visit to South Asia under cover of which he wants to slip into Peking from Pakistan. If the South Asian visit was announced at short notice like June 15, it would lead to immense speculation in the press not only

here but everywhere abroad. He pointed out that he received the Chinese reply from me only on the night of June 2 when the special courier arrived with it here and thus it left too little time to quietly announce a routine trip to South Asia.

3. Therefore President Nixon had decided that the Kissinger trip should be postponed to the early days of July when he will go via the Pacific to Bangkok and drop into Delhi and Islamabad after spending at least 48 hours in Delhi (otherwise the Indians will wonder why he stayed as much as 3 days in Pakistan).

4. Accordingly he will arrive in Rawalpindi airport in his Presidential Boeing by noon on Thursday July 8 from Delhi. He will fulfill any official programme we draw up for him for the rest of that day.

5. At early dawn the next morning (Friday July 9) he would like to leave for Peking in our Boeing. He would come back from Peking in our aircraft by the afternoon of Sunday July 11 to leave Rawalpindi nonstop for Paris that very night.

6. Kissinger also wants to inform Peking that he would not bring an interpreter. He would expect that the Chinese would look after this matter and he would be glad to use their interpreter.[3]

7. He is not bringing his own tele-communication equipment with him to Peking because if he uses it, he feels the Russian will be able to find out that someone in Peking is trying to contact Washington.

8. While in Pakistan Dr. Kissinger and his four aides would like to be together in the same building. I said we would put him and his aides in the Presidential guest house in Rawalpindi. He thanks you for this and requests that you kindly inform the Chinese authorities that while in Peking he

hopes they would also keep him and his four aides together in the same building. (Also that he loves Chinese food[4] and would like to see some of the sights of Peking incognito).

9. Kissinger wants the Chinese authorities to confirm above dates for his visit to Peking as urgently as possible because he would like to make an announcement about his South Asian trip quickly. He would be grateful if you could request the Chinese authorities to kindly accept the dates suggested above for the Peking visit as any alternative dates would be extremely difficult to arrange from the point of view of camouflaging the visit. As soon as the Chinese authorities would confirm the dates, Kissinger proposes to announce publicly 'a credible and visible object' for his trip to South Asia.

10. I enclose a note prepared by me about the detailed arrangements for his secret Peking trip mentioned to me by Kissinger.

11. I have typed this letter and its enclosures myself.

[The letter was headed 'Top Secret. By Safe Hand.']
    The third document—a note of Hilaly's discussions with Kissinger—covered the details of Kissinger's overt and covert programme for Islamabad:

1. Dr Kissinger suggested the following programme for our consideration regarding his Pakistan and Peking visit:

(a) after his arrival in Rawalpindi about noon on July 8 we can make an open official programme for him to discuss matters of mutual interest with President, M.M. Ahmad and Foreign Secretary. (I presume after official talks are over, President would like to have Kissinger come for drinks before he attends a small dinner party at President's House if President would like to hold one for him.)

(b) perhaps next morning at early dawn he could leave Rawalpindi airport openly for Sargodha military airport to get into the PIA Boeing waiting there to take him to Peking or direct from Rawalpindi secretly in the PIA Boeing for Peking. He thinks that since the Pakistan press and the international press will be told that on completion of his official talks by evening of July 8, he (Kissinger) is being taken (along with Farland) by M.M. Ahmad or some other Pakistani official for two days of rest and recreation to a Pakistani resort (whatever place you fix), we will obviously have to stage some such open departure for him from Rawalpindi in a Pakistani Fokker Friendship plane to Sargodha or if he goes direct from Pindi to Peking, we will still have to send Farland and the Pakistani host to the above resort by a small plane to show that Kissinger left Pindi for the resort. He will ask Farland to stay in the Pakistani resort till Sunday afternoon along with our representative so that the diplomatic corps, U.S. Embassy staff and the Pakistani public and press think he was actually away in that resort with Farland during the time he was in Peking.

(c) Kissinger proposes to take with him to Peking four male aides. (Please note Farland is not being included in his party.) These aides will be accompanying him from Washington.

(d) On Sunday July 11 afternoon, when he returns to Islamabad from Peking, Farland and our man can also return from the Pakistani resort to Pindi as if they brought back Kissinger with them. He is afraid of any one from the diplomatic corps or American Embassy, Islamabad, getting to know the secret. He therefore wants to make it quite clear to the U.S. Embassy staff that during his visit to Pindi he will be entirely with us Pakistanis and that except for Ambassador Farland, he does not want to take with him on his rest and recreation trip any member of the American Embassy staff in Islamabad because his four aides will be with him during this two days holiday.

(e) to ensure the above, he would like to stay in the President's guest house in Rawalpindi and not in Ambassador Farland's house or a hotel.

2. Kissinger thinks that if he can leave Pindi by the PIA Boeing at dawn on July 8 he should be in the secret airport near Peking by 1 p.m. that day. <u>He wants us to kindly inform the Chinese authorities that he will be entirely with them all the time he will be in Peking</u>. He does <u>not</u> want to contact any foreign mission in Peking during his stay there because he does want any foreign mission in Peking to know of his visit.

3. For the return journey he would like to leave Peking any time after 11 a.m. on Sunday July 11 which should bring him to Rawalpindi by 6 p.m. or so, on that day. There should be no secrecy about his departure from Rawalpindi for Paris subsequently that evening (after a few hours) so that the diplomatic corps, American Embassy staff and our press will know that he came back from the Pakistani resort to Rawalpindi that evening and actually left for Paris that night.

4. Kissinger also told me that if he sends a White House official from here to Islamabad to tie up all these details about his flight from Islamabad to Peking and back with our officials, there was much risk of leakage from U.S. Embassy in Islamabad. Therefore the U.S. Government would be grateful to us if we could fly out our official whom you would be entrusting with the task of finalising Kissinger's complicated programme of his secret visit to Peking and back. He assumes this official would belong to our Intelligence Services in order to ensure that he would treat the whole matter as of top secrecy. I would suggest that he should come here fully prepared with our plan for the whole of this operation—timings, place where Farland and the Pakistani companion supposed to be taking Kissinger for his two days rest in a Pakistani resort will be staying on 9 and 19 [*sic*]

July, exact flight time and schedule of flights from Pindi to Peking and back, accommodation for our Boeing crew for the two nights in Peking (Kissinger hopes that our crew will also not contact our Embassy in Peking while they are there and the Chinese authorities will agree to look after them. This means our Boeing crew will also have to be sworn to secrecy.[5]) Since Kissinger and his party will be only five persons, a minimum crew for the PIA Boeing is all that will be necessary.

5. I trust I will be informed as to who will be the person who will come here for this purpose to discuss and complete all these arrangements with the White House officials concerned. I would suggest that he should arrive here as quickly as possible after consulting not more than one high-powered PIA official on a top secret basis about the timing and other requirements necessary for the Boeing flight to Peking and back after two days stay there.

6. I would request the name and arrival details of this official should be telegraphed to me in cypher (restricted) as I want to make special arrangements to receive and put him up without the knowledge of my staff here.[6]

The following day, on 6 June 1971, Hilaly wrote separately by hand to President Yahya, sharing observations which he could not for obvious reasons include in his 'open letter' of 5 June. Hilaly recounted:

When I asked Dr. Kissinger if he would like a high level Pakistani official to accompany him on his visit to Peking, he asked whether we wanted to be present at his talks with the Chinese. Obviously, as disinterested friends offering good offices, I said we would leave this decision to him. If he wanted our assistance or our presence at the talks, we would be happy to oblige—not otherwise.

Kissinger replied he did not know how the Chinese would take it. Perhaps it was best if he met the Chinese without a third party being present. I could see quite clearly he had no desire to have one of us at his talks with Premier Chou En Lai or his aides. (You will have noticed that he does not want to take even Ambassador Farland with him to Peking.)

Incidentally Kissinger told me he has never handled a gun in his life, so no American will believe we are telling the truth if we say that the two days holiday he is taking when he disappears from Pindi on 9th July was for hunting in the northern areas. (I am mentioning this just in case some one had the idea of saying so.) He does not fish. Therefore it would be best if we say he is going away for those two days to rest and relax after his South Asian trip. If you are thinking of sending Farland & M.M. Ahmad (or some other Pakistani companion) to Chitral or Hunza, etc., it can be added that he went to see our huge mountain peaks—everyone will believe that a foreigner has a desire to see the 'mysterious' Hunza valley—Shangri La as it is called.

With best wishes & with prayers from all of us that your health should stand the terrible strain that recent events have caused. The next few months are even more important.

P.S. As you must be aware I made all the arrangements for Field Marshal Ayub Khan[7] who was successfully operated upon on 10th of last month. He left the hospital five days ago and is convalescing in a small hotel on the outskirts of the same city (Cleveland).

Hilaly consigned his letter to the waiting Foreign Office courier Mr Bashir Babar who left Washington with it on 6 June. Despite all the precautions by the White House, the Presidency at Islamabad and the Prime Minister's office in Beijing, it would appear from the memoirs of Mr Sultan Khan that they could not insure against human fallibility, for according to him, while waiting for a flight connection at London airport, Mr Babar fell asleep and missed his flight. 'Yahya Khan was extremely upset at the delay and continued to inquire daily as to what Babar was up to!'[8]

Mr Babar's recollection of the return journey differs. He had to reschedule his departure from Washington and came not via London, as originally planned, but via Amsterdam. As there was an eight hour wait at Amsterdam before the connecting flight to Karachi, he was offered a tour of the city or a rest at a nearby hotel. He chose the latter as he was reluctant to leave the airport premises with such a precious consignment in his custody.[9] He decided to take a nap, was woken up in time and caught the outward flight. When he reached Rawalpindi, he was driven straight to the Presidency where he found an impatient President and even more agitated Foreign Secretary waiting for him.

The substance of Kissinger's message brought by Mr Babar was conveyed to Premier Zhou Enlai through the Chinese Ambassador on 9 June 1971, at 7.15 p.m.

President Nixon received your Excellency's message through me on 2 June, through a special courier. It was not therefore possible for him to announce Dr Kissinger's visit to South East Asia at short notice like June 15, as it would have lead to immense speculation in the press, not only in the U.S. but also abroad. He would now come to Pakistan on his return trip from South East Asia on 8 July. Leaving Islamabad early morning of 9 July, I could slip him into Peking and bring him back to Islamabad by the evening of 11 July. I hope and trust that this arrangement will suit Your Excellency.

I have also been informed that Kissinger will not bring an interpreter.

Kissinger and his party of four and also the crew of my aircraft will be entirely with the Chinese Govt. and no one else, including Pakistan Embassy will be brought in the picture.

Kissinger is looking forward to the kind invitation of Your Excellency and he has stated that he loves Chinese food and would like to see some of the sights of Peking, incognito if possible.

President Nixon requests the confirmation of these dates as soon as possible so that an announcement could be made of Kissinger's visit to South East Asia.

[The name 'Sultan' appears on the bottom left of the message.]

Yahya Khan acknowledged the receipt of the message through a cypher telegram sent from the Foreign Office. Marked 'Top Secret. From President for Ambassador Hilaly only', it read:

Reply to message sent by you through Bashir Babar has been received today. New dates and time suggested in the message have been fully accepted. Please suggest that proposed announcement by the other side may now be made. Actual text of message being sent by bag. Please acknowledge.

The Chinese on their part responded with accommodating swiftness. In a message dated 11 June 1971 from Premier Zhou Enlai to President Nixon, delivered orally by the Chinese Ambassador to President Yahya Khan on 12 June, the Chinese side confirmed:

President Nixon's message transmitted by President Yahya Khan on June 9, 1971 has been received. Premier Chou En-lai agrees to change the time of Dr. Kissinger's visit to Peking to July 9th to 11th, 1971. The Government of the People's Republic of China will make all the necessary preparations accordingly.'

[A fair copy of this message was sent to Hilaly on 14 June 1971.]

In a separate section of the message, intended for President Yahya, Premier Zhou Enlai specified in more detail the programme regarding the aircraft etc. to be used by Dr Kissinger:

1. Premier Chou En-lai thanks President Yahya Khan once again for the efforts Your Excellency has made in transmitting messages between China & the U.S.

2. We agree to postpone the trial flight and envisage it may be changed to end July. The specific time will be decided upon later. By that time we shall send our navigators by special plane from Peking straight to an airport designated by the Pakistani side in Islamabad. Our special plane will fly back immediately after its arrival, whereas our personnel will remain in Pakistan to await the trial flight of the Pak Boeing aircraft. Upon its arrival in Peking, the Pak Boeing aircraft may return on the same day after refuelling, and our navigators will go back to Pakistan by the same aircraft to await orders in Islamabad.

3. In order to greet Dr. Kissinger, we shall send appropriate officials to Islamabad on the return flight of the Pak Boeing aircraft, who will then accompany Dr. Kissinger to Peking by the same plane. We request President Yahya Khan to kindly study whether it is appropriate and advise us on Your Excellency's opinion.

4. In order to maintain secrecy, it is suggested that the personnel of China, the U.S. and Pakistan be all exempted from passports & visas for the above journeys.

President Yahya sent the message to Hilaly with his opinion:

The above message seems to clinch the issue finally. You must have received Sultan's letter by bag by now in which details to be arranged by us are mentioned. Please assure the Friend that absolutely fool-proof arrangements will be made by us and he need have no anxiety on this count. I will be expecting Dr. Kissinger arriving Islamabad midday July 8, 1971.

Please deliver the message above the line immediately and signal confirmation on their part and any reactions.

The next communication we have is Hilaly's Top Secret cypher message No. C-521 for President Yahya, dated 22 June 1971. Its contents read:

Kissinger called me yesterday [11 June 1971] to convey personal appreciation of President Nixon to you for 'great service to peace and to mutual relation you are rendering by acting as a true friend of two parties'. He said he is looking forward very much to meet[ing] you in Rawalpindi on July 8th.

2. He is leaving Washington for Bangkok via Pacific on July 1st. Will arrive Delhi July 6th evening and Rawalpindi midday July 8th. Because he does not want to cause unnecessary speculation in India about reason for staying longer period in Pakistan he is at present informing India that he is leaving for Paris on 10 July. After reaching Pakistan it will be announced on July 9th evening that owing to slight indisposition in Nathiagali to which we have taken him for rest and relaxation he is obliged to postpone his departure by 24 hours. He asked if we had any objection to this device. I said none. Other party may be informed about this so that when Kissinger's programme is published here in the next two or three days they may not think that his visit to them is being shortened. Original dates both for Rawalpindi visit and for other places stand. Kissinger also wants you to designate official to whom message on routine matters regarding his

visit could be delivered by Farland. I presume it will be Foreign Secretary or your Military Secretary. Grateful if you would let me know by telegram. More detailed letter follows by tomorrow's bag.

The Chinese Ambassador was informed of this at midday on 24 June 1971.

The letter Hilaly referred to in his cypher message was a two-pager with three annexures, all faultlessly typed by him personally. The letter, dated 22 June on Embassy of Pakistan letter-head, contained eight paragraphs. Hilaly began:

This is further to my cypher telegram No. C-521 of today just sent informing you about what Kissinger told me yesterday evening on his return from the Florida White House.

2. He explained that as he is reaching New Delhi on July 6 evening and will be leaving on July 8 at midday for Rawalpindi (less than 24 hours stay), the Indians might get suspicious as to why he is planning to stay as much as 3 days in Pakistan (midday July 8 to evening of July 11). [Yahya Khan scribbled in the margin: 'No more than 24 hours!'] Therefore in announcing his programme here within the next two or three days he will state that he is leaving Pakistan for Paris on July 10 instead of July 11. He, however, intends to stick to the original programme which means that he will be returning from Peking afternoon of July 11 and departing for Paris that night after seeing you (he asked me whether you would like to see him after his return from Peking. I said you would).

3. What he wants us to do is that on the 9th evening we should announce in Rawalpindi that he has extended his stay in Nathiagali by one more day owing to indisposition and

will now return to Rawalpindi only on July 11 afternoon to take off immediately for Paris. I said we had no objection. We would announce the shorter programme to begin with, subsequently amending it to permit an extra day's stay as originally settled.

4. I am surprised at the arrangements he is making to ensure secrecy for his Peking visit. (names of those coming with Kissinger to Pindi are given in Appendix "A"). He is bringing not only a "double" for himself but a "double" also for his personal assistant Winston Lord[10] whom he is taking with him to Peking in addition to John Holdrich[11] [Holdridge], Richard Smyser and a security man and possibly a woman stenographer with a typewriter. The "doubles" who it appears look very much like Kissinger and Lord have to be taken to Nathiagali by us along with Ambassador Farland and whoever you designate to go with this party to Nathiagali. Therefore the Chinese have to be informed now that the Kissinger party will consist of six persons including Kissinger and not five as originally intimated. (Listed in Appendix "B"). He is assuming that M.M. Ahmad will kindly agree to take the dummy party to Nathiagali under the pretext that M.M. Ahmad will continue his discussions with Kissinger in Nathiagali. (Perhaps Ahmad can drive up to Nathiagali with the party and return after a few hours.)

5. In all probability, as I may have to come to be present at the Kissinger's meetings in Rawalpindi, (if the situation here will permit me to leave on this hurried visit), presumably I will also have to go Nathiagali for those 2 days with Farland and the "doubles". (Appendix "C" shows list of Americans going to Nathiagali).

6. Accommodation for the crew of the presidential aircraft and for Mr. Harold Saunders[12] (White House aide) all of whom will stay back in Rawalpindi from July 8 to 11 will be made by Farland.

7. Kissinger has requested that the crew of the PIA Boeing to Peking may be told to fix some special code name for the aircraft for purpose of keeping in touch with Rawalpindi and Peking air towers during the flight. It appears that if they use the PIA number and usual call sign certain countries who are listening to these calls between aeroplanes may find out that a PIA Boeing special flight is being made between Rawalpindi and Peking on that trip.

APPENDIX "A". NAMES OF THOSE COMING WITH DR. KISSINGER TO RAWALPINDI.

1. Dr. Henry A. Kissinger.
2. "Double" of Dr. Kissinger
3. Mr. Halperin (Private Secretary to Dr. Kissinger)
4. Mr. Winston Lord (Dr. Kissinger's aide)
5. "Double" of Mr. Lord.
6. Mr. John Holdrich (Dr. Kissinger's aide)
7. Mr. Richard Smyser (Dr. Kissinger's aide)
8. A security man.
9. Mr. Harold Saunders (White House aide)
10. Woman's [sic] stenographer.

APPENDIX "B": LIST OF THOSE GOING WITH DR. KISSINGER TO PEKING.

1. Dr. Kissinger
2. Mr. Winston Lord
3. Mr. John Holdrich
4. Mr. Richard Smyser
5. A security man
6. Possibly the woman stenographer.

[Kissinger's notes on his team were: 'I chose my associates: John Holdridge, a Foreign Service Officer and China specialist who handled East Asia on the NSC staff;

Dick Smyser, another Foreign Service Officer and Vietnam expert on my staff; Winston Lord, formerly of State and Defense and now my special assistant on the most sensitive matters, a trusted confidant and close friend.'[13] In the event, there was no female stenographer. Kissinger relied instead on Winston Lord to check the translations and to take notes. The six man group included two security agents—Jack Ready and Gary McLeod. The latter are identifiable in the photograph showing Kissinger and his party touring the Forbidden City in Beijing, reproduced in Kissinger (1979), between pp. 744–5.]

The third Appendix 'C' contained the names of the decoy party which would travel to Nathiagali and stay there over the weekend:

APPENDIX "C": LIST OF AMERICANS GOING TO NATHIAGALI.

1. Ambassador Farland
2. Mr. Halperin.
3. "Double" of Dr. Kissinger.
4. "Double" of Mr. Lord.
5. Pakistani to be nominated by President as host of the party (Mr. M.M. Ahmad?)
6. Ambassador Hilaly?

P.S. It will be noticed that the Pakistani who is going along with the American party to Nathiagali in the capacity of host entertaining the Americans will have to be selected with great care as he will have to be told why the operation has been mounted.

Hilaly followed his letter of 22 June with a tracer sent the next day, at Dr Kissinger's specific insistence:

Dr. Kissinger has asked me to inform you as follows:

When he sent for Ambassador Farland last month at the California White House to tell him that certain top secret messages would be exchanged between President Nixon and yourself in the coming months (and that he may be utilised either by President Nixon or by yourself to transmit such messages) he did not reveal to Farland that he intended to visit Peking itself. Therefore until now, while Farland knows that secret messages are being exchanged between Washington and Peking about Kissinger holding secret talks with the Chinese in Pakistan, he is not aware that Kissinger's destination is Peking during the coming secret trip nor that he will meet Chou En Lai himself.

2. Kissinger requests that if you have not informed Farland about the above specified destination or the above specific person, it would be preferable not to reveal these two names to Farland for the present and to keep the matter of the destination and the exact person vague.

Despite this, a final message of reassurance was sent by Washington through Ambassador Farland, delivered by him at noon on 29 June and communicated to the Chinese Ambassador an hour later, at 1.00 p.m., on the same day. The message concerning the Five Nuclear Power Disarmament Conference read:

1. The U.S. Government wishes the Government of the People's Republic of China to know that it will not answer the Soviet Government with respect to the question of the Five Nuclear Power Disarmament Conference until Dr. Kissinger has discussed the matter during his forthcoming visit.

2. The U.S. Government will maintain the strictest secrecy with respect to Dr. Kissinger's forthcoming trip regardless of whatever speculation may occur in the U.S. Press or elsewhere.

3. During his visit, Dr. Kissinger will be empowered to work out with the Government of the People's Republic of China the substance and form of a possible subsequent announcement of his trip.

Hilaly's keenness to extract mileage from the White House for use of the Pakistani channel comes to the fore in the letter he sent to Dr Kissinger on 1st July, which happened to be his last day in office before embarking on his South East Asian trip and secret visit to Peking. Hilaly wrote:

As you were so busy and pressed for time last evening, I do not remember whether I impressed upon you sufficiently the following matters which are of utmost importance to us during the next few months:

(i) that the Indians should not think that any military operations contemplated by them to take the refugees back into adjoining East Pakistan territory under the protection of their army would be tolerated by us as not amounting an invasion of East Pakistan and

(ii) that if they (a) continue to threaten to go to war against us and (b) continue to state publicly that the refugees cannot go back to East Pakistan until Sheikh Mujibur Rahman is released and allowed to install his Awami League Government in that province, the refugees in fact will not go back. Therefore, for heaven's sake, India must stop making such threats and such statements if she genuinely desires to get rid of her three million refugees. In other words she cannot have it both ways, that is, continue to demand Pakistan should make impossible political concessions in East Pakistan and get rid of the majority of the refugees.

2. Nothing President Yahya's Government can do to bring the refugees back to East Pakistan—particularly Hindu refugees—can succeed unless India stops saying in effect that a political settlement in East Pakistan has to meet with her approval.

3. Kindly read the enclosed latest nationwide address of President Yahya before you reach Pakistan.

Wishing you a most successful trip. Warm regards till we meet in Pindi.

To President Yahya, on 2 July, Hilaly sent a copy of his letter to Kissinger and the following note:

I briefed Kissinger personally before he left last evening on his South East Asia trip what we would like him to do for us in New Delhi. But to make doubly sure he should not forget, I sent him the enclosed letter before he left.

2. I will be coming to Pindi on July 6 evening to be there when Kissinger arrives. I would be grateful if you could favour me with an interview on July 7 (evening if possible). Kissinger told me he would value any suggestion you might make as to what tactics he should adopt to make the Chinese in Peking co-operate and improve his credibility.

Dr Kissinger's South-Asian trip went according to plan. In New Delhi, he held discussions with the Indian Prime Minister Mrs Indira Gandhi on 7 July 1971. They were not specific to the animosity developing in the subcontinent but more global in their range: 'I told Indira Gandhi that we would continue to oppose unprovoked military pressure by any nuclear power, as enunciated in the Nixon Doctrine.'[14]

When he reached Islamabad the next day after his talks in New Delhi, Kissinger privately cautioned his Pakistani hosts about the mood of belligerence he had encountered across the border. His views were summarised, probably by Sultan Khan, in a handwritten note on paper headed 'Government House, Nathia Gali', initialled and dated '9/ 7 [July]':

> Dr. Kissinger has stated that in Delhi he found a mood of bitterness, hostility and hawkishness, and he came away with an impression that India was likely to start a war against Pakistan. United States has conveyed a strong warning to India against starting hostilities but she may not pay heed, thinking that present hostile attitude of press and Senate against Pakistan offers her a good opportunity.
>
> Under these circumstances it might make all the difference between war & peace in the sub-continent if China could make clear to India directly as well as through the important visitor that China's interest in Pakistan's integrity and security remains unchanged and that if Pakistan is subjected to aggression China will not remain a silent spectator.[15] In other words a reiteration of China's position conveyed in the open message of April 1971, now appears very timely.
>
> I would request you to kindly convey the above to His Excellency the Premier in continuation of the talk I had with you on 7 July.

Yahya Khan's preoccupation and priority though was with arranging Kissinger's programme. On President's House note-paper, the following programme was outlined by his Military Secretary and approved with a tick against each item:

3 July (or 4 July)

0600 1. Chinese navigators arrive by Illyushin aircraft. The
         aircraft either returns the same day (refuelling) or
         next day.
      2. Chinese navigators stay with Chinese Embassy.

5 July

Evening flight   Boeing (normal) arrives Chaklala. Parks
(1740)   in PAF area for the night.

Same evening: 1. Meeting Chinese navigators & Pilot &
                  Navigator.
               2. Fix code word for flight
               3. No normal chitchat which gives away PIA
                  for recognition.

6 July

0430   1. Boeing leaves on test flight.
(Time?)   2. Returns the same evening with Chinese
                  Navigators and Chinese delegation.
               3. Taxis to PAF area—Delegation received
                  by Chinese Ambassador and taken to
                  Chinese Embassy.

7 July   What happens to Boeing?

8 p.m.   President receives Chinese delegation for
                 dinner.
                 List of guests—foreign and own.

8 July

Midday	K with a party of 10 arrives Received by M.M. Ahmad + Sultan + Farland openly and taken to President's Guest House (who stays where?) Lists Air Force Two—Crew?
Afternoon—	M.M. Ahmad and Sultan meet Kissinger officially.
7 p.m.	K. calls on President—Main House.
8.30 p.m.	1. K stays on for dinner. Other guests arrive for dinner. 2. List for dinner.
Evening flight	Boeing arrives and parks PAF area.

9 July

0330	Umar[16] goes to Chinese Embassy with 3 or 4 cars and conveys party to PAF area and embarks them by 0400.
0400	Sultan takes K + 5 in Pakistan cars + goes to PAF area and embarks them straight to Boeing, introduces the two parties + returns.
0430	Boeing takes off.
0930	Arrive destination (12.30 C.T.)
0700	K's double + party leave Govt. House for Nathiagali

1. President Nixon with President Agha M. Yahya Khan, at Lahore, 2 August 1969. It
was during this visit that Nixon first suggested to Yahya Khan that Pakistan should
act as the intermediary between the US and the People's Republic of China.
Also visible in the photograph standing on the left of President Yahya Khan are his
Military Secretary Major-General M. Ishaq and his brother Agha Mohammed Ali,
then Inspector-General of Police. His son Ali Yahya Khan (in a dark suit) is visible
in the background behind Nixon.

2. Agha Hilaly, Pakistan's Ambassador to the US, receiving Dr Henry Kissinger on his arrival at Chaklala airport, Rawalpindi, on 8 July 1971.
In the background on the left are Joseph Farland, US Ambassador to Pakistan at the time, and on the right Sultan M. Khan, then Pakistan's Foreign Secretary.

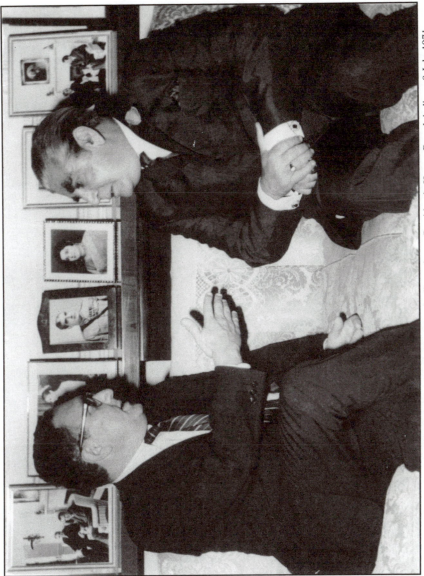

3. President Agha M. Yahya Khan and Dr Henry Kissinger in discussion at President's House, Rawalpindi, on 8 July 1971.

4. President Richard Nixon, Dr Henry Kissinger (then Assistant to the President for National Security Affairs) and Pakistan's Ambassador to the US Agha Hilaly, photographed in the Oval Office of the White House. (Photo: Courtesy Ambassador Agha Hilaly.)

Evening—	Announce indisposition.
10 July	Halt destination
11 July	
11 AM C.T./ 8 AM P.T.	Take off.
1300 (P.T.)	Land Chaklala—Taxi straight to PAF area K + party drive to President's House +Main House. Lunch or talks.
17.20	Leave Guest House for Chaklala. Press.
1800	Take off. Seen off by Sultan and M.M. Ahmad. Umar main coordinator throughout.'

In consonance with the programme, Dr Henry Kissinger and his party left New Delhi on 8 July 1971 and landed at Rawalpindi airport as scheduled, just before noon. *Dawn* reported: 'Soon after his arrival, Dr. Kissinger drove to Islamabad for lunch with U.S. Ambassador Joseph Farland. He later conferred with the Ambassador and members of his staff.' It informed its readers that 'Dr. Kissinger will be spending the day tomorrow in Nathiagali, where he will take rest, it was officially announced today. It will, however, be a working holiday and senior officials who are to meet him in Islamabad will now be holding discussions with him in Nathiagali.'

Kissinger's narrative of the day he spent in Islamabad before embarking on his historic journey carries an immediacy and authenticity that could have come only from a person who stood centre stage in the drama about to unfold. His account begins: 'My visit to Islamabad followed the script to the letter. There was a lunch at Ambassador Farland's residence with what was left of the embassy staff, a meeting with President Yahya, a briefing at the Embassy, and then again a private dinner with Yahya and senior associates.'

He continues: 'During the course of his dinner in my honour Yahya began implementing our plan. My stomach-ache became a topic of general conversation.[17] He announced loudly that the heat of Islamabad would impede my recovery; he urged that I repair to Nathiagali, a private estate adjoining a presidential guest house in the hills above Murree. When I demurred, he insisted, against all the evidence of history, that in a Moslem country the host's not the guest's wishes are decisive. He was so convincing that one of my Secret Service agents who overheard the conversation immediately arranged for a colleague to make an "advance" visit to the hill station. Around midnight the agent called in great distress; he had looked over the guest house and found it unsuitable. There was nothing to do other than to ask the Pakistanis to detain the hapless agent in Nathiagali until my return from Peking.'[18]

One of the last messages Kissinger received from his Chief was the information that on the eve of his secret journey to Beijing, on 8 July 1971, almost two years since Nixon had initiated a probe to the Chinese through Yahya Khan in August 1969, the President thought fit to inform his Secretary of State William Rogers that the Presidential Assistant for National Security Affairs Henry Kissinger would be visiting China on his behalf. Even at this late stage, Nixon held back. He told Rogers that Kissinger was going 'in response to an invitation [he] had received while in Pakistan.'[19]

Secretary Rogers' reactions were not likely to disturb Kissinger, even had he been aware of them. Although he slept fitfully, he was awake early next morning to board the PIA aircraft for Beijing.[20] Luck or perhaps something stronger was on his side. Standing in the darkness at the Pakistan Air Force controlled area of Chaklala airport was an experienced Pakistani journalist Mirza Farrukh Humayun Beg, a stringer for London's *Daily Telegraph*. Beg had served as a press attaché in various Pakistani embassies abroad and was known amongst his colleagues as having connections with the intelligence agencies. He claimed to have watched Kissinger board his flight[21] and quickly returned home to file a story with the *Telegraph*. The story, which would certainly have made Beg's career and perhaps marred Kissinger's, and could have qualified as the 'most important' scoop since the Second World War, was killed somewhere between Islamabad and London—perhaps deliberately.[22]

NOTES

1. Kissinger (1979), p. 727. An abridged version of the message has been reproduced by him.
2. An abridged version of Nixon's message was published in Kissinger (1979), pp. 727–8.
3. This was a subtle confidence building measure, supported by Kissinger's awareness that his assistant Winston Lord spoke fluent Chinese.
4. Kissinger later disclosed that he put on two pounds in weight during this trip and five during the subsequent one in October 1971.
5. 'The anxiety about the PIA crew leaking information remained and General Omar [Umar] decided to appeal to them in the name of patriotism and Pakistan's national interest, to forget, until the official announcement, that they had made the trip to Beijing. It worked and they kept the secret'. Khan (1997), p. 268.

6. In the event no official was sent from Pakistan.
7. Former President Ayub Khan (Chief Martial Law Administrator, October 1958–February 1962; President, February 1962– February 1969) was Yahya's predecessor. He had gone to Cleveland for a heart operation.
8. Khan (1997), p. 251.
9. For the return journey, Mr Babar had sewn the letter into the jacket pocket himself.
10. Winston Lord's looks belied his age, prompting Chairman Mao to comment when they met during Nixon's 1972 visit that 'he was so young, younger than the interpreters.' Burr (1998), p. 87.
11. Hilaly has mis-spelt the name of Holdridge throughout his memo as Holdrich.
12. 'Hal Saunders (who was familiar with the plan) remained in Islamabad to discuss bilateral issues with Pakistani officials and to handle emergencies.' Kissinger (1979), p. 741.
13. Kissinger (1979), p. 730.
14. Kissinger (1979), p. 736.
15. See also Khan (1997), p. 269.
16. Major General Ghulam Umar, Secretary, National Security Council (1970–1971).
17. Kissinger's stomachache was to recur in Beijing seven months later, in February 1972, during Nixon's visit. At the conclusion of the third round of conversations between Nixon and Zhou Enlai on 23 February 1972 in Beijing, the following exchange takes place when Zhou suggests that the aides might have to forgo a trip to the Great Wall in order to conclude the communiqué:
'Prime Minister Chou: As for the communiqué, I understand they have already agreed to meet. They should start working and will have to skip the Great Wall.'
President Nixon: I think he (Dr. Kissinger) is too lazy and does not want to climb the Wall again.
Dr. Kissinger: I have a stomach-ache.
President Nixon: If he has a stomach-ache, there will be a story in the press.'
(*Memorandum of Conversation No. 3,* 23 February 1972, p. 41. National Security Archive, Washington).
18. Kissinger (1979), p. 739.
19. This would not be the last indignity Secretary Rogers would have to endure at the hands of either Nixon or Kissinger. When

President Nixon met Chairman Mao in February 1972, he was deliberately excluded by Nixon (abetted by Kissinger) from the American party received officially by Mao. Kissinger later repented, describing the act as 'fundamentally unworthy' (Kissinger [1979], p. 1057).

20. In Rashomon-style, two participants in the same event had differing recollections of the same incident. Holdridge (1997), p. 53 describes Kissinger driving to the airport 'hunched over in the back of a red Volkswagen Beetle with a hat pulled down over his head and wearing dark glasses', but defers to Sultan M. Khan's more prosaic recall that the car was in fact a blue Datsun, driven by Sultan Khan himself (see Khan [1997], p. 264).

21. The apron at Chaklala airport where the PIA aircraft used by Kissinger was parked was in the military section and therefore off-limits to civilians. It had also been kept dark without lights.

22. See Isaacson (1992), p. 344. Isaacson suggests that Beg's editor in London, 'assuming that Beg was drunk, listened politely then spiked it.'

4

POLO IN BEIJING

When Dr Henry Kissinger boarded the PIA aircraft at Chaklala airport in the early hours of Friday, 9 July 1971, he was introduced in the privacy of the cabin to the Chinese emissaries sent by Premier Zhou Enlai to accompany him to Beijing. The senior-most among them was Zhang Wen-Jin, then head of the West European, American and Oceanic Department in the Chinese Foreign Ministry.[1] With him was Tang Ling Bing from the Protocol Department, Wang Hai-Rong, a lower level official from the Chinese Foreign Ministry but also Mao's niece,[2] and the second woman in the team—Tang Wen Sheng, known better to Kissinger by her western name of Nancy Tang.[3] (Having been US-born—in Brooklyn—Nancy Tang possessed a qualification nature had denied Kissinger: she was eligible to stand for the American presidency.) Because of their closeness to Chairman Mao, their presence was especially significant. They had all flown in two days earlier and had been waiting in the Chinese Embassy in Islamabad.

In his memoirs, Dr Kissinger makes the astonishing admission that, prior to boarding the flight to Beijing, he had never met any Chinese Communists before.[4] In a sense, he did not need to. The briefing book prepared for him by the indefatigable Winston Lord and his team was comprehensive to a fault. Kissinger had shown it—a 'big black tome'—to President Nixon who read its summary carefully, marking his observations and comments on the front page.[5] A code name was determined for the secret trip—appropriately it was Polo after Marco Polo, the Venetian traveller and writer who had visited China exactly seven centuries earlier, between 1271–75.

Sultan Khan recalled that early morning rendezvous clearly: 'Dr. Kissinger and I left the Guest House at 4 am followed by two staff cars with his aides and security guards. We reached the Air Force part of Chaklala Airfield shortly afterwards, and the guard, who had been alerted to expect our cars, waved us through after checking my identity. General Omar had already arrived with Ambassador Chang Wen-Chen [Zhang Wen-Jin] and others whom he had picked up from the Chinese Embassy and seated them in the Boeing. Dr. Kissinger and others boarded immediately and the plane was airborne at 4.30 am sharp, as planned.'[6]

The aircraft was in the command of a senior PIA pilot Captain M. Taimur Baig, who had flown the inaugural PIA flight between Karachi and Shanghai in 1964. Baig recalled that for the Kissinger trip he had been given a destination—Beijing—but no information of the name of the passenger, except that it would be a VVIP. He was informed by his purser of Kissinger's presence on the aircraft. When the plane neared Beijing, Capt. Baig was told by the airport control that he was not to land at Beijing airport but to proceed to a military airfield nearby, where although unfamiliar with its runway he achieved a smooth landing.

Meanwhile in Pakistan, Ambassador Farland and Kissinger's assistant David Halperin took the doubles of Dr Kissinger and Winston Lord by car to Nathiagali, where they were joined by Sultan Khan. Dr Kissinger's double went to his room and remained out of sight. Later the same evening, though, Sultan Khan received an urgent message: 'I received word that "Dr. Kissinger", confined upstairs, was not well and wished to see me. He complained of severe stomach pains, and on questioning, I found that he had consumed half-a-dozen mangoes in lieu of lunch.'[7] Efforts were made quickly to find a doctor, preferably one who had never heard of Henry Kissinger and therefore would not be able to recognize him or detect the double. One was found and by morning the surrogate Dr Kissinger had been restored to ill health.

The newspapers covered Kissinger's indisposition with reports fed by official sources. *Dawn*, for example, in its issue of 10 July reported: 'Dr. Henry Kissinger stayed on in Nathiagali today cancelling a round of talks with President Yahya Khan, a visit to GHQ and a dinner arranged for him by the President. General Abdul Hamid Khan, Deputy Chief Martial Law Administrator and Chief of Staff, Pakistan Army, called on Dr. Kissinger and had lunch with him in Nathiagali. An official handout this evening said that Dr. Kissinger was "slightly indisposed".' Hal Saunders, who had remained in Islamabad, was reported as holding meetings on Pakistan's economic plans and food situation with Pakistani officials, including M.M. Ahmad, Economic Advisor to the President and Mr M.H. Sufi, the President's Advisor on Food and Agriculture and Kashmir Affairs.

'Dr. Kissinger' remained indisposed the next day as well, though well enough to receive the Defense Secretary Mr Ghiasuddin Ahmad.[8] A rumour that one of the reasons for Dr Kissinger sequestering himself in Nathiagali may have been to facilitate a secret meeting with Mujibur

Rahman's aide Kamal Hossain[9] helped divert attention of the media from discovering the truth.

In Beijing, Kissinger spent the weekend of 9–11 July 1971, undoubtedly the most exhilarating weekend of his life, primarily in discussions with a man whom he warmed to immediately—the ineffably erudite Zhou Enlai. Six years later, in January 1977, Kissinger had occasion to recall that first trip when he reminisced with his successor-designate as Secretary of State Cyrus Vance and Ambassador to the UN Huang Hua, one of those deputed by Zhou Enlai to receive him at Beijing airport on his first arrival.

Ambassador Huang: Time flies so fast since the first secret trip.

Mr. Vance: I remember very well reading about the trip when the story broke back here. It was a very exciting moment in history.

The Secretary: I think it was the single most exciting moment for me, that trip to China.[10]

Unless the Chinese release their transcripts (which must surely exist) of the discussions held between their Premier and the visiting American emissary, Kissinger's memoirs shall remain the most detailed source of information available to historians about his visit. He was clearly overawed by Zhou Enlai, describing him as 'one of the two or three most impressive leaders' he had ever met, the others being Charles de Gaulle and Mao Zedong. To Kissinger, Zhou Enlai appeared 'urbane, infinitely patient, extraordinarily intelligent, subtle', moving through their discussions 'with an easy grace that penetrated to the essence of our new relationship as if there were no sensible alternative.'[11]

The obstacle Kissinger feared might obstruct his aim to find common ground between himself and his Chinese hosts was of course the spectre of Taiwan and the Taiwan Straits. Both he and Zhou Enlai acknowledged that since the objective of Kissinger's visit was not to resolve the intractable problem of Taiwan, which had bedevilled Sino–American relations since the end of the Second World War, but to prepare for a visit by Nixon, they could afford to leave that narrow agenda to their aides. They freed themselves from this chore and dilated instead on subjects which stimulated their minds, discussing topics which held graver consequences for them and because of them for the rest of the world. Although Taiwan remained an insoluble question, to Kissinger, 'the answer was to discuss fundamentals: our perceptions of global and especially Asian affairs, in a manner that clarified our purposes and perspectives and thereby bridged two decades of mutual ignorance. Precisely because there was little practical business to be done, the element of confidence had to emerge from conceptual discussions. Chou and I spent hours together [seventeen in all] essentially giving shape to intangibles of mutual understanding.'[12]

On the 10th morning, the American party were taken on a tour of the Forbidden City, after which Kissinger and Zhou had another round of talks in the Fukien room,[13] named after the province facing Taiwan. (Neither Kissinger nor his Sino expert Winston Lord caught the nuance, until Zhou explained it to them later.) A lunch of Beijing duck[14] helped to ease an awkwardness during the negotiations, and after the meal, a proposal was made almost casually by Zhou for a Presidential visit in 1972. A short debate ensued, and then it was agreed that the spring of 1972 would be mutually acceptable.

During the evening Zhou had to absent himself as he was needed to host a dinner for a visiting dignitary, whose identity for understandable reasons was not disclosed by Zhou to Kissinger. It was in fact the North Korean leader Kim Il Sung. Zhou promised to return at 10.00 p.m. to look at the draft communiqué. When he did come, he left the actual drafting to Huang Hua and spent the next hour with Kissinger, discussing primarily India and Germany. 'His basic point,' Kissinger noted, 'was that India had been the aggressor against China in 1962; there was a great danger of the same policy's being applied to Pakistan in 1971.'[15]

The final draft communiqué was accepted by both parties with surprisingly little fuss and within time (as the deadline for the visit could not be extended beyond forty-eight hours), and so, on 11 July, as planned, after lunch Kissinger and his party left in the same PIA Boeing aircraft that had brought them to Beijing. Zhou Enlai, a storehouse of sage Chinese sayings, might have given the departing Kissinger the same advice he proffered to another guest once: 'Go slowly, come back quickly'.[16] Kissinger returned to Beijing for a second visit in October and seven more times before the end of 1975.

Kissinger and his party landed at Chaklala airport at 3.00 p.m. on 11 July, where they were met by General Ghulam Umar.[17] After making a detour to connect with the road from Murree to maintain the illusion that he had spent the weekend at Nathiagali, Kissinger paid a brief call on President Yahya Khan, who as he put it 'was boyishly excited ecstatic about having pulled off this coup.'[18] During this brief stop in Pakistan before returning home, Kissinger had sent a personal message of thanks to

Premier Zhou Enlai. Written on President's House notepaper, Kissinger wrote in block capitals:

TO PREMIER CHOU-EN-LAI

ON BEHALF OF MY COLLEAGUES AND MYSELF I WANT TO THANK YOU FOR YOUR WARM AND GRACIOUS RECEPTION. UPON OUR RETURN WE SHALL WORK [*TO IMPLEMENT ALL THE UNDERSTANDINGS WE*—deleted and substituted by] TO STRENGTHEN FRIENDSHIP AND COOPORATION [*sic*] BETWEEN OUR PEOPLES

KISSINGER

By 6.00 p.m. Kissinger was aboard his own plane *en route* to Tehran. During the journey he sent a single word coded message—*Eureka*—to President Nixon at San Clemente signifying success of his mission. He met Nixon there on 13th evening and spent almost two hours de-briefing him on his momentous trip.

On 15 July, simultaneously, the communiqué agreed between Kissinger and Zhou Enlai in Beijing was read out simultaneously in the United Sates and in China, announcing that 'Premier Chou en-lai, on behalf of the Government of the People's Republic of China, has extended an invitation to President Nixon to visit China at an appropriate date before May 1972. President Nixon has accepted the invitation with pleasure.'[19]

The modalities for the Presidential visit were understood by the two parties to be a visit of up to five days (Nixon stayed in China for almost eight days, arriving in Beijing on Monday 21 February 1972 and leaving from Shanghai the following Monday 28 July), one other city besides Beijing (Nixon visited Hangchow and Shanghai), small official and press delegations[20] and an agenda which would cover anything each party would wish to bring up without binding one or the other.

Kissinger prepared a twenty-one page report on 17 July for the President,[21] describing his visit and the talks he had held with the Chinese leadership, and also his perception of the matters which were of concern to them. On returning to the White House, Kissinger wrote to Yahya Khan, a fortnight after he said goodbye to him in Islamabad,[22] thanking him personally for the role he played in bringing the two countries together. Kissinger's letter of 26 July 1971 and that of President Nixon of 7 August were sent by General Alexander Haig to Agha Hilaly for his scrutiny before being issued. Hilaly made a small but significant correction and returned them to Haig on 23 July with a handwritten note saying, 'The alterations I have taken the liberty to suggest have been shown by me in their separate photocopies below the originals. I have deliberately left some of the alterations incomplete (marked by a dotted line) to enable Dr Kissinger to say just what he wants to say about my little assistance as obviously I could not draft my own certificate.'

Dr Kissinger's final letter read:

Dear Mr. President:

I have so many reasons to thank you that it is difficult to know where to begin.

First of all, there is the vital role that you[23] played in establishing communications between us and the People's Republic of China. Your initiative and discretion made possible the reliable and secure contacts that led to my visit and the President's forthcoming trip. You were also well served, Mr. President, by your representative here.

Ambassador Hilaly's part in this operation vividly demonstrated why he has compiled so remarkable a diplomatic career.[24]

Then, the skill, tact, efficiency with which your officials carried out my secret mission were nothing short of brilliant. I hope you will pass on my deep appreciation, and that of the President, to all those who realized this venture, including some of your closest advisers, and the captain and crew of your airplane. My colleagues and I were greatly moved by the historic nature of our flight and the care and warmth with which we were treated as we crossed some of the world's highest mountains.

Mr. President, the deepest thanks go to you who led and orchestrated the entire enterprise. I shall always remember your generosity in our talks on July 8 when you insisted on setting aside the massive problems that your country faces and concentrating instead on my visit to Peking. In addition, I enjoyed, and profited from, my too brief stay in Pakistan itself, the conversations we had, and the gracious Pakistani hospitality.

Your efforts and those of your colleagues have made indelible contributions to my personal experience, the foreign policy objectives of the United States, and I believe, the goal of peace in the world.

With warm regards

Sincerely,

Henry A. Kissinger

Richard Nixon also wrote a handwritten personal letter to Yahya Khan. His letter—the last from a Head to a Head—conveyed the extent of his feelings and gratitude:

August 7, 1971.

Dear Mr. President—

I have already expressed my official appreciation for your assistance in arranging our contacts with the People's Republic of China.

Through this personal note I want you to know that without your personal assistance this profound breakthrough in relations between the USA and the PRC would never have been accomplished.

I wish you would extend my personal thanks to your Ambassador in Washington and to your associates in Pakistan for their efficiency and discretion in handling the very sensitive arrangements.

Those who want a more peaceful world in the generations to come will forever be in your debt.

Dr. Kissinger joins me in expressing our deepest gratitude for the historic role you played during this very difficult period.

Sincerely,

Richard Nixon

The Chinese version of these historic events has remained embedded in their archives. Occasionally, one obtains a glimpse into their view of that momentous weekend of 9–11 July 1971. Mr Zhang Wen-Jin, leader of the delegation which had received Kissinger in the PIA Boeing aircraft on 9 July, then accompanied him to Beijing, and was a participant in all the major meetings with Kissinger, wrote fifteen years later in the *People's Daily* issue of 21 May 1986: 'The arrangement was so perfect that we may use the Chinese expression to describe it, "Just like a heavenly garment, wholly seamless it is".'[25]

NOTES

1. Later Deputy Foreign Minister.
2. Identified as the grandniece of Mao Zedong's mother. See Holdridge (1997), p. 54.
3. Interpreter to Chairman Mao Zedong.
4. Kissinger (1979), p. 741. Neither apparently had his accompanying Secret Service detail. Zhou Enlai told Ambassador Hilaly subsequently that when Kissinger and his team boarded the PIA aircraft, the two American security guards, upon seeing the Chinese delegation, immediately pulled out their handguns, cowboy-style. (Hilaly to FSA, interview, 21 November 1999.)
5. Kissinger (1979), p. 734.
6. Khan (1997), p. 264. In fact, Dr Kissinger was driven to Chaklala airport by Col. (later Brigadier) Muzaffar Malik, then Director General, National Security Council. In an interview with the author FSA, he recalled driving Dr Kissinger alone without any security detail, in his red Volkswagen car. This would seem to corroborate John Holdridge's recollection of that rather distinctive vehicle (see Holdridge [1997], p. 530).
7. Khan (1997), pp. 264–5.
8. *Dawn* issues of 9 and 10 July.
9. Sultan refers to him as Kamaluddin Ahmad (see Khan [1997], pp. 265–6). Even Zulfikar Ali Bhutto thought Kamal Hossain was in Nathiagali striking a deal over Bangladesh with Kissinger (see Raza [1997], p. 105).
10. Burr (1998), p. 482.
11. Kissinger (1979), p. 745.
12. Kissinger (1979), pp. 745–6.
13. Zhou Enlai confirmed to Nixon during his 1972 visit that the room in which they were holding their meetings was in fact the

Fukien room, 'the same one in which he had entertained Dr. Kissinger in 1971 and had the duck lunch.' (*Memorandum of Conversation No. 2*, 22 February 1972 (National Security Archive, Washington).

14. Holdridge describes how Zhou Enlai takes Kissinger and his party to the kitchens to see where and how the Peking duck was prepared. They found the kitchens empty, save for one lone PLA soldier who looked understandably 'stunned' at seeing the foreign guests. (Holdridge [1997], pp. 59–60.)

15. Kissinger (1979), p. 751.

16. Quoted in Khan (1997), p. 212.

17. The PIA crew was kept incommunicado by General Umar at the Intercontinental Hotel, Rawalpindi to ensure secrecy, just as during their three days in Beijing they had been kept secluded in a Government guest house. Capt. Baig recalls them being treated with great courtesy and attention. To occupy their time, the PIA crew was shown a propaganda film which the Chinese thought might be of particular national interest to them—that of the Sino-India conflict of 1962.

18. Kissinger (1979), p. 755. He also says that Yahya was 'enthralled by the cops-and-robbers atmosphere of the enterprise' (p. 739). Kissinger was no less animated by the adventure. Sultan Khan recalled him as returning from his trip to Beijing 'bubbling with excitement'. Yahya spoke of him as 'being extremely relieved and grateful'.

19. Zulfikar Ali Bhutto, when asked to comment, said: 'Naturally it is a welcome and inevitable development and it will yield salutary results.' *Dawn*, 16 July 1971.

20. The Americans were keen to have a large press corps. Necessarily, coverage of the July visit by Kissinger had been given restricted coverage by only Chinese photographers. Before leaving Pakistan, Kissinger sent the following typed message to his Chinese counterpart:

'Due to the demand here, we have agreed to the release of three of the photographs that you so kindly provided during my visit. These three are: (1) The Premier and Dr. Kissinger (alone) shaking hands; (2) The Premier and Dr. Kissinger (alone) sitting down; and (3) Chinese officials greeting Dr. Kissinger at the airport on his arrival. Please feel free to release any of the photographs or T.V. films from your end that you deem appropriate.'

These photographs have been reproduced in Kissinger (1979), between pp. 744–5.

21. Record Group 59, Dept. of State Records, 1970–73. I am indebted to Mr William Burr, National Security Archive, Washington, for drawing my attention to this report and for generously making a copy available.

22. Kissinger and Yahya Khan were not to meet again. Kissinger wrote of their final meeting: 'I was probably responsible for the last pleasant day Yahya had before he was overthrown as a result of the India-Pakistan war in December of that year.' (Kissinger [1979], p. 739.)

23. The original text read 'the vital role you and Ambassador Hilaly played'. Hilaly deleted his own name as it suggested a level of equivalence between Yahya Khan as the President and himself as his ambassadorial representative. He told General Haig in a note: 'I think de-linking my name from the President's is required by protocol in our part of the world, but I most grateful both to President Nixon and Dr Kissinger for the honour they did me in linking it in the first instance.' (Agha Hilaly to General Alexander Haig, 23 July 1971.)

24. Hilaly suggested the words 'You were well served, Mr. President, by your representative here. Ambassador Hilaly's assistance...', leaving it to Henry Kissinger to complete the sentence in his own words.

25. Khan (1997), p. 271.

5

AFTERMATH

There is 'too much turmoil under the heavens', Zhou Enlai told Kissinger during their private discussions in Beijing, a concern Kissinger took seriously enough to include in his report to President Nixon. The final report prepared by Kissinger for Nixon was longer than Kissinger's threatened book on German poetry. When Nixon met Zhou Enlai himself in February the following year, he told him that when 'Dr. Kissinger returned from his trip in July and in October, the total number of pages in the transcript was over 500.'

"That must have been quite a tiring thing to read about," Zhou Enlai replied.

"It was very interesting. I think the Prime Minister will find this hard to believe, but except for General Haig and these gentlemen here [John Holdridge and Winston Lord], and Dr. Kissinger of course, I am the only one who has seen these 500 pages. I have read the whole 500. We have provided a sanitised memorandum of conversation for others[1]—I am talking here in great confidence—who are on the trip with us, like Secretary of State Rogers and Assistant Secretary Marshall Green. This is because they need to have some of this information in order to do their work."[2]

The 'turmoil' which was causing such disturbance in the minds of the Chinese leadership was the looming crisis in the subcontinent following the results of the general elections in Pakistan. While the conduct of the polls in December 1970 were never questioned by any of the contesting parties, the results were found unarguable by Sheikh Mujibur Rahman's Awami League party which had a clear majority by winning 160 seats out of the total of 300. The same results were found disagreeable by Yahya Khan who had hoped for a hung Parliament with him continuing as President. And they were found unacceptable by the vociferous Mr Zulfikar Ali Bhutto whose Pakistan People's Party held 81 (just over 26 per cent) of the seats, but was adamant in his resolve not to sit in Opposition. Mr Bhutto's centripetal view, which transformed into party policy, was that he had not resigned from Ayub Khan's cabinet four years earlier, in June 1966, simply to eke out a political career on the wrong side of power.

The dilemma confronting Yahya Khan as the President of a country with two dissenting wings was clearer than its solution. The Awami League had won its 160 seats entirely in the East Wing of the country, but had no representation at all in the West Wing. Mr Bhutto's PPP, along with other West Pakistani parties (42) and Independents (15), polled negligible votes in East Pakistan but had a significant presence in the West. The real issue was not who should head the National Government or who should sit in the Opposition. The issue was not even whether that Government should function henceforth from Dhaka, in the way that all previous governments had operated from the west wing, first from Karachi, and later Islamabad. The critical unspoken issue was whether there was any justification in maintaining the two-wing theory, the unworkable residue of the two-nation theory which had been the basis for the partition of the subcontinent in August 1947. Few politicians involved in the debate chose to discuss this issue or the modalities of its inexorable consequence. They preferred rhetoric to action. Frustrated and un-assuaged representation led to civil insurrection in East Pakistan, organized by the Awami League. In a misguided and ultimately misunderstood attempt to maintain the fiction of national unity between the two wings of the country, united by a common name but divided permanently by a common enemy India, Yahya Khan (acting with the tacit encouragement of Bhutto) initiated military action by the Pakistan army in East Pakistan.

The ferocity and brutality of the suppression resulted in an exodus of millions of refugees into the neighbouring and already overcrowded Indian state of West Bengal. The figures escalated from over 119,000 in April 1971 to half a million by end April, and by 21 May had swelled to 3.4 million.[3] A figure as high as 10 million was circulated by Mrs Indira Gandhi in the international community,[4] large enough for her to regard it as grounds for supporting their return, if necessary, by a force as military as the one that had driven them out. Using Bengali officers and troops who had defected from East Pakistan, a Mukti Bahini force was created, aided and supported by the Indian army. To those who understood Mrs Gandhi's mind, nursing as it did a hostility, incubated in 1947, to the very idea of Pakistan, a war in the subcontinent with the aim of liberating East Pakistan, and making it an independent sovereign state, was inevitable. The only things which needed resolution were when should such a war start, who was likely to come to the aid of whom, and what would be the fate of West Pakistan?

These questions were the recurring elements of the discussions at a global level throughout the summer of 1971, between the Indians and the Russians compacted on one side, and the Pakistanis and the Americans and the Chinese in a loose formation on the other.

Although Nixon and Kissinger at the White House could, within limits, and in fact did, conduct a personal sort of state-craft which often ran counter to the official position of the US Government acting through its Department of State, they were cautious enough to maintain in public a semblance of conformity with official US policy regarding the subcontinent, which was one of even-handed neutrality. When Kissinger intended to visit Islamabad and to use it as the springboard for his secret trip to Beijing, he was careful to plan a stay no longer (officially at least) than the number of days he had allotted for New Delhi. Nixon's famous tilt towards Pakistan though was interpreted as a clear message of his personal preference for Pakistan. If this tilt heartened Yahya Khan in Pakistan, it was anathema to Mrs Indira Gandhi in India. The Indian attitude was made clear to Dr Kissinger when he visited New Delhi before flying to Pakistan. During Kissinger's talks with Mrs Indira Gandhi and members of her government in New Delhi, he was left in no doubt about her militaristic plans to sever Pakistan nor about her intransigence in implementing them.

Hours after leaving New Delhi, Kissinger tried to convey to President Yahya and his coterie of appointed advisers in Islamabad the danger they faced in both wings of their target country. 'I urged them to put forward a comprehensive proposal to encourage refugees to return home and to deny India a pretext for going to war,' he wrote. 'I urged Yahya and his associates to go a step farther in the internationalization of relief by admitting the United

Nations to supervise its distribution. And I recommended the early appointment of a civilian governor in East Pakistan.'

Yahya's reaction appeared encouraging on the surface, but as Kissinger recognized, he was a servant rather than a master of events: 'Yahya was a bluff, direct soldier of limited imagination caught up after the convulsion in East Pakistan in events for which neither experience nor training prepared him. He made grievous mistakes.'[5]

Three months before Kissinger's visit, the Foreign Secretary Sultan M. Khan had held serious discussions on the East Pakistan situation with Premier Zhou Enlai in Beijing. In April 1971, accompanied by Lieutenant-General Gul Hassan Khan,[6] he went to Beijing and met Zhou privately, without the Pakistani Ambassador Mr K.M. Kaiser present. Zhou Enlai knew that Mr Kaiser came from East Pakistan and therefore might feel 'embarrassed' by what they would have to discuss.

First, Sultan made a statement. He conveyed his President's disappointment, shared by the people of Pakistan, at the 'lack of response' from China, whom they regarded as 'a reliable friend.' They expected that China 'would categorically express its solidarity and support for Pakistan ... and make its stand clear in a formal statement.'[7]

Premier Zhou Enlai replied by saying that while the situation initially had appeared hopeful, the army action instituted in East Pakistan on 25 March had been perceived as a setback. Better informed than Sultan Khan himself was about the situation in East Pakistan (particularly in regard to the brutalities and genocide) Premier Zhou summarised the advice he wished to convey to Yahya: '...if a feeling of estrangement was to be minimised, then the Pakistan army had to have a greater 'mix' of officers and soldiers from both wings; and the pressing need for political action within the country, with a gradual reduction of the involvement of the military in the governance of the country.'

That China was siding with a military dictator against a popularly and democratically elected party (the Awami League) was an irony not lost on Sultan Khan nor spoken of by Zhou Enlai. Instead, Zhou reaffirmed China's support for Pakistan's unity by issuing an appropriate statement through the *People's Daily* and gave practical aid in equipping two army divisions. Sultan Khan left Beijing clearer about China's unambiguous position: 'China never, during these or subsequent talks, held out any possibility of coming to Pakistan's aid with her armed forces.'[8]

In any case, China never acted in a hurry, its Premier told Sultan Khan. It studied every aspect of a situation before expressing itself. But when it did, it did so with the force of a clenched fist (one of Zhou's favourite analogies). Therefore, when Zhou and Kissinger met in Beijing later in July, Zhou's precis of events in the subcontinent was candid, frank and at times trenchant. From the memorandum prepared for Nixon by Kissinger after his visit, Zhou made the following exposition of China's perception of the situation in the subcontinent:

Chou described the South Asian subcontinent as a prime area of 'turmoil under heaven'. This was because India had long ago, under Nehru, adopted an expansionist policy, not only committing aggression against Pakistan but against China as well.

Chou went into great detail to outline the development of the hostile relationship between China and India. This began, he said, when the Indians became aware in 1959 that the Chinese had built a road across Indian-claimed territory between Sinkiang and the Ali region of Tibet—but how could this have been Indian territory when the Indians weren't even aware when the road was built?

The Indians had then attacked a Chinese military post in this region, but had lost heavily because the Chinese position was uphill from where the Indians were and was strongly fortified. But world opinion (including Khrushchev)[9] felt that the Chinese must have started hostilities because of the heavy Indian losses. The Indians had also used force against the Chinese in other areas. The culmination was the Sino-Indian war of 1962.

Chou made the following points:

• India was responsible for the present turmoil in East Pakistan. It was supporting Bangla Desh and had allowed a Bangla Desh 'headquarters' to be set up on Indian territory.

• In the light of Indian expansionist ambitions, India would use any military aid—such as that given by the USSR—for aggressive purposes. Chou acknowledged that we were not giving military assistance to India, but said that one had to keep the consequences of any aid in mind.

• China would stand by Pakistan in the present crisis. This position began to develop with a rather low-key remark at dinner the first night that China 'could not but take some interest in the situation', and ended with a request to me at the end to convey assurances of Chinese support to President Yahya Khan.

• I told Chou that we were trying very hard to discourage an Indo-Pak war. I assured him that we were bringing all the influence we could to try to prevent a war from developing. Chou said this was a good thing, but he inferred that we might not be able to do too much because we were 10,000 miles away. China, however, was much closer. Chou recalled the Chinese defeat of India in 1962 and hinted rather broadly that the same thing could happen again.

The Chinese detestation of the Indians came through loud and clear. Conversely, China's warm friendship for Pakistan as a firm and reliable friend was made very plain. The lesson that Chou may have been trying to make here was that those who stand by China and keep their word will be treated in kind.[10]

(Kissinger was to comment on this trait during his meeting with Ambassador Huang Hua a year later. Kissinger told him: '...it was my first acquaintance with the Chinese style of diplomacy, in which I learned, as I have said publicly, that Chinese word counts, that one can rely on what our Chinese friends say.'[11] Zhou Enlai, on another occasion, put it more succinctly: 'Zhou Enlai does not eat his words.'[12])

Within five days of this conversation with Kissinger, Premier Zhou sent the following message of support on 14 July 1971 to Yahya Khan though the Chinese Ambassador in Islamabad. A handwritten note on President's House note pad records the full text:

<u>Chinese Ambassador gave orally on 14 July 1971.</u>

Premier Chou En-lai requested me to convey Chairman Mao's regards to Kissinger and Premier Chou En-lai's thanks to President Yahya Khan.

Some progress. Info about talks later.

2. Chou En-lai indicated to Kissinger: In case India invades Pak, China <u>will</u> not be idle spectator but will support Pak. It is hoped that U.S. will exert influence to persuade India. Pakistan will not provoke India ......[illegible line] However should India recklessly take such a step, she will reap her own bitter fruit.[13]

Kissinger indicated that the impression he gained in Delhi attack was possible. U.S. will look on this with great disappointment. In case Mily. Action—the U.S. will express strong opposition openly.

Words were welcome, but Yahya Khan and his beleaguered army needed armaments and supplies. On 30 July, Ambassador Agha Hilaly wrote to President Yahya Khan:

Yesterday President Nixon gave separate interviews both to me and to Ambassador Farland. Farland saw him first and told me subsequently that President Nixon had discussed the East Pakistan [issue]. Farland added that he would see[k] an interview with you on his return to Islamabad and tell you all about it.

2. The gist of what President Nixon said to me about East Pakistan situation is contained in my telegram to Foreign Secretary No. C-611 dated July 30 which I trust you have seen. I could not include the following points in that telegram as I thought President Nixon intended that they should be conveyed to you more confidentially. He appeared to me genuinely concerned about the difficulties you were facing in East Pakistan. He told me repeatedly that he wanted to help you as much as possible and though the entire American public, press and Congress were enraged, owing to exaggerated stories of army brutality and the flood of refugees entering India, he would do his best to see that the Congress did not tie up his hands by putting a complete embargo on military and economic aid. He was sending messages to friendly governments to similarly avoid succumbing to the pressure of their public opinion and press. His delegation at the U.N. would also be instructed to cooperate to [with] us to the maximum extent possible. He wished he could do more but he had to cope with the massive opposition mounted by the American news media and Congress. From this point of

view your acceptance of all offers of international assistance to get the refugees back into East Pakistan was absolutely right. He was very happy when you offered (presumably referring to your interview with Neville Maxwell) to invite the U.N. to station observers on both sides of the border which India had declined. In his discussions with important Congressmen he found that this offer of yours had greatly impressed them. As a result American public opinion was beginning to take note of the rigidity of India's attitude.

3. President Nixon went on to say that he was profoundly grateful to you for your invaluable help and advice in putting him in touch with the Chinese. The manner in which the Kissinger trip had been organised by you and your aides showed that in spite of all the difficulties in maintaining secrecy during negotiations of the highest international importance these days, it was still possible for some governments who possessed patriotic officials of high integrity to respect the confidential nature of such negotiations (at this stage he paid me a few compliments for my own part in this affair). He said you had not merely helped a friendly government like the U.S. but the whole international community and the cause of world peace by bringing about U.S.-Chinese discussions. Kissinger had found your advice as to how to deal with the Chinese extremely useful. By his own experience with you and your officials he (Nixon) was not surprised that Kissinger had found that the Chinese held you in high esteem.

Gradually though the Indian diplomatic offensive was beginning to constrict and then close Pakistan's options. On 9 August 1971, India signed a Twenty-Year Treaty of Peace, Friendship and Cooperation with the Soviet Union. Exactly three months earlier, Zhou Enlai had cautioned Sultan Khan that the USSR would do all they could to aggravate the situation. 'They have no principles and act merely according to the changing needs of the diplomatic situation. At the time of Tashkent Conference [in January 1966], they wanted one Pakistan; now they want to split it up.'[14] Kissinger assumed that the Russians were taking advantage of Pakistan's difficulties and China's public association with it, 'to humiliate China and to punish Pakistan for having served as intermediary.'[15]

When Zhou Enlai and Kissinger met again in Beijing between 20–26 October 1971, Kissinger 'detected less passion and more caution' in Zhou than he had displayed during their previous encounter in July that year. Kissinger reported to Nixon:

Chou opened up by saying that the situation was very dangerous and asked for our estimate.

I made the following points:

• At first India had a reasonable complaint about the political and economic burden of the refugees coming from East Pakistan. We had moved to meet this problem by providing one-half of the foreign relief to refugees in India, or nearly $200 million.
• However, India might be tempted to take advantage of the crisis as a means of settling the whole problem of Pakistan, not just East Pakistan. The Indian strategy apparently could be to change abruptly the situation in East Pakistan so as to shake the political fabric of West Pakistan.
• I then outlined U.S. policy and the steps we had taken to support Pakistan in the consortium, debt relief, and other bilateral areas. I emphasized our total opposition to military action by India. I added that we had urged the Russians to exercise restraint. They had told us they were trying to do so, but we were not sure whether this was in fact the case.
• We thought there was a danger of hostilities in the near future.

• Finally, I outlined our proposal that both forces withdraw
their troops from the border and that Yahya make some
political offers so as to overcome hostile propaganda and
make it easier to support him in the U.N. and elsewhere.

Chou thanked me for this information and said that he wished
to discuss this issue the next day in more detail. He
commented that Tito had been persuaded to the Indian view
by Mrs. Gandhi, and this plus Soviet support would increase
the risk of Indian miscalculation.

I then stated that we had no national interest in East
Pakistan and only wanted the political solution there to reflect
the will of the people. We had made many proposals to India
to separate the refugee problem from the political evolution
in a way that would not prejudge the future. However, India
had not responded.

Chou commented that the Soviets were exploiting the
situation, as part of the general strategy of exploiting
contradictions in Asia so as to free their hand in Asia. He
thought this was 'a very stupid way of thinking.'

Perhaps significantly, Chou, despite his promise, never
came back to this subject. This might be partly due to the
fact that we spent so much time on other subjects. However,
there were opportunities to raise South Asia again in our
subsequent meetings if Chou had really wanted to.

In any event, China still stands clearly behind Pakistan.
However, I believe the PRC does not want hostilities to break
out, is afraid of giving Moscow a pretext for attack, and
would find itself in the awkward position if this were to
happen.

Chou surely recognized from my presentation that we have
too great stakes in India to allow us to gang up on either side.
Nevertheless he did not attempt in any way to contrast their
stand with ours as demonstrating greater support for our
common friend, Pakistan.[16]

Kissinger summarised his discussions with Zhou Enlai on this incendiary issue in one pithy paragraph:

South Asia. The PRC doesn't want any subcontinent hostilities any more than we do. Indeed the Chinese seemed more sober about the dangers than they did in July. Chou reaffirmed their support for Pakistan and their disdain for India. In turn I made it clear that while we were under no illusions about Indian machinations and were giving Pakistan extensive assistance, we could not line up on either side of the dispute.[17]

The 'disdain' for India felt by the Chinese was paralleled by barely concealed hostility exhibited both by President Nixon and by Mrs Indira Gandhi during their meeting in Washington in November 1971.

Although Nixon held an opinion that out of all the world leaders he had met, 'Nehru would certainly rank among the most intelligent. He could also be arrogant, abrasive, and suffocatingly self-righteous, and he had a distinct superiority complex that he took few pains to conceal.'[18] He had also met Mrs Gandhi in 1953 when she was her father's hostess and found her 'charming and graceful [.] When I encountered her years later, however, when she was Prime Minister and I was President, there was no doubt that she was her father's daughter. Her hostility toward Pakistan was, if anything, even stronger than his.'[19]

Nixon shared this perception of Mrs Gandhi's genetic inheritance with Premier Zhou Enlai who, in their meeting together in 1972, expressed the thought that it was a 'great pity' that she had taken 'as her legacy the philosophy of her father embodied in the book Discovery of India.' He asked Nixon whether he had read it. Kissinger, sensing that his President had not, intervened with: 'He was thinking of a great Indian Empire?' Zhou replied: 'Yes, he was thinking of a great Indian Empire—Malaysia, Ceylon, etc. It would probably also include our Tibet. When he was writing that book he was in a British prison, but one reserved for gentlemen in Darjeeling. Nehru told me himself that the prison was in Sikkim, facing the Himalayan mountains. At the time I hadn't read the book, but my colleague Chen Yi[20] had, and called it to my attention. He said it was precisely the spirit of India which was embodied in the book. Later on when I read it I had the same thought.'[21]

The meetings between Mrs Gandhi and President Nixon at the White House were spread over two days, on 4 and 5 November 1971. Had they been two days shorter, neither of the participants would have complained.

The meetings started on a palpably false note. As Nixon recalled, with more generosity than accuracy, Mrs Gandhi complimented him 'highly' on the way he was winding down the war in Vietnam and on the boldness of his Chinese initiative. Nixon responded by drawing her attention to the 'uneasy situation' in East Pakistan and how important it was for India not to do anything to exacerbate it. To this Mrs Gandhi gave the disarming, implausible reply that India was not motivated by anti-Pakistani attitudes. 'India has never wished the destruction of Pakistan or its permanent crippling. Above all, India seeks the restoration of stability. We want to eliminate chaos at all costs.'[22]

Kissinger's more detailed account of the Nixon–Gandhi meetings, which he termed 'a classic dialogue of the deaf', depicts her expressing admiration for Nixon's achievements in Vietnam and China, 'in the manner of a professor praising a slightly backward student.'[23] Nixon, according to Kissinger, found her condescending and hypocritical. She listened to him 'without a single comment, creating an impregnable space so that no real contact was possible.'[24]

At one stage, when she did speak, she talked of the creation of Pakistan with an ember of resentment still glowing after over a quarter of a century of the independence of India and Pakistan from the British and from each other.

Her father, she averred, had been blamed for accepting partition. And there was an element of truth, she said, in an often-heard charge that India had been brought into being by leaders of an indigenous independence movement while Pakistan had been formed by British collaborators who, as soon as they became "independent", proceeded to imprison the authentic fighters for Independence.[25] Pakistan was a jerry-built structure held together by its hatred for India, which was being stoked by each new generation of Pakistani leaders. Conditions in East Pakistan reflected tendencies applicable to *all* of Pakistan. Neither Baluchistan nor the Northwest Frontier properly belonged to Pakistan; they too wanted and deserved autonomy; they should never have been part of the original settlement.[26]

The following day, Nixon kept Mrs Gandhi waiting for forty-five minutes before receiving her. The denouement was predictable. During the meeting itself, she spoke about every topic except Pakistan and what she proposed to do with it.

The war between India and Pakistan began on 22 November 1971 with an all-out offensive by India against East Pakistan. On 24 November, Mrs Gandhi admitted that three days earlier Indian troops had crossed the international border. On 2 December, Pakistan invoked the rusty 1959 bilateral agreement between the US and Pakistan. Another similar act of desperation was the attack launched by Yahya Khan on the western front. Kissinger, who understood Yahya Khan better than many, interpreted his decision for Nixon: 'In simple-minded soldierly fashion he decided...that if Pakistan would be destroyed or dismembered it should go down fighting.'[27]

Such a vital decision, though, like the war itself, was no longer in his inept hands. Countries which had an interest in maintaining a balance in the subcontinent, which had conferred in July and in October in Beijing, shifted their conference to a safe house managed by the CIA in New York's East Side. Meeting in the evening of Friday, 10 December 1971, Kissinger and Huang Hua assessed the situation. The transcripts of their discussions reveal:

Dr Kissinger: ...Our judgment is if West Pakistan is to be preserved from destruction, two things are needed—maximum intimidation of the Indians and, to some extent, the Soviets. Secondly, maximum pressure for the cease-fire.

At this moment we have—I must tell you one other thing—we have an intelligence report according to which Mrs. [Indira] Gandhi told her cabinet that she wants to destroy the Pakistani army and air force and to annex this part of Kashmir, Azad Kashmir, and then to offer a cease-fire. This is what we believe must be prevented and this is why I have taken the liberty to ask for this meeting with the Ambassador.

One other thing. The Acting Secretary of State—the Secretary of State is in Europe—called in last night the Indian Ambassador [L.K. Jha] and demanded assurance that India has no designs, will not annex any territory. We do this to have legal basis for other actions. So this where we are.

Ambassador Huang: We thank Dr. Kissinger very much for informing us of the situation in the subcontinent of India-Pakistan, and we certainly will convey that to Prime Minister Zhou Enlai.

The position of the Chinese Government on this matter is not a secret. Everything has been made known to the world. And the basic stand we are taking in the UN is the basic stand of our government. Both in the Security Council and the plenary session of the General Assembly we have supported the draft resolutions that have included both the cease-fire and withdrawal, although we are not actually satisfied with that kind of resolution. But we feel that the draft resolution which had the support in the Security Council and especially the one which we voted in favor of in the General Assembly, reflect the overwhelming majority of the small and medium countries.[28]

After listening to the re-statement of the Chinese position, a refrain with which he was already familiar, Kissinger responded with a directness that demanded concentration:

Mr. Ambassador, we agree with your analysis of the situation. What is happening in the Indian sub-continent is a threat to all people. It's a more immediate threat to China, but it's a threat to all people. We have no agreement with the British to do anything. In fact we are talking to you to come to a common position. We know that Pakistan is being punished because it is a friend of China and because it is a friend of the United States.

But while we agree with your theory, we now have an immediate problem. I don't know that history of the people's revolution in China nearly as well as you do. I seem to remember that one of the great lessons is that under all circumstances the Chinese movement maintained its essence. And as an article in the Chungking negotiations makes clear, it is right to negotiate when negotiations are necessary and to fight when fighting is necessary.

We want to preserve the army in West Pakistan so that it is better able to fight if the situation rises again. We are also prepared to attempt to assemble a maximum amount of pressure in order to deter India. You read the *New York Times* every day, and you will see that the movement of supplies and the movement of our fleet will not have the universal admiration of the media, to put it mildly. And it will have the total opposition of our political opponents.

We want to keep the pressure on India, both militarily and politically. We have no interest in political negotiations between Pakistani leaders and East Pakistani leaders as such. The only interest we possibly have is to get Soviet agreement to a united Pakistan. We have no interest in an agreement between Bangladesh and Pakistan.

We are prepared also to consider simply a cease-fire. We are prepared also to follow your course in the UN which most of my colleagues would be delighted to do and then Pakistan would be destroyed.

If we followed your course of insisting on cease-fire and withdrawal and do nothing then Pakistan will be destroyed, and many people in America will be delighted. If you and Pakistan want this then we will do it. That is no problem for us. That is the easiest course for us.

So we will ... we agree with your analysis completely. We are looking for practical steps in this issue which happens to be a common fight for different reason. We will not cooperate with anyone to impose anything on Pakistan. We have taken a stand against India and we will maintain this stand. But we have this problem. It is our judgment, with great sorrow, that the Pakistan army in two weeks will disintegrate in the West as it has disintegrated in the East. If we are wrong about this, we are wrong about everything.[29]

On 15 December, five days after these discussions in New York, the East Pakistan forces again offered a cease-fire. During the intervening five days, pressure had been mobilised to prevent the destruction of what remained of Pakistan—its west wing, a Pakistan even more truncated than its founding father M.A. Jinnah had envisaged.

'Next day Mrs. Gandhi offered an unconditional cease-fire in the west,' Kissinger wrote. 'There is no doubt in my mind,' that it was a reluctant decision resulting from Soviet pressure, which in turn grew out of American insistence, including the fleet movement and the willingness to risk the summit. This knowledge stood me in good stead when Vietnam exploded four months later. It was also Chou En-lai's judgment, as he later told Bhutto, that we saved West Pakistan. The crisis was over.'[30]

Meeting in February 1972, for the third time in less than a year, Kissinger and Zhou Enlai could exchange notes on this crucial test of their scheme to synchronise their actions, despite their differing political philosophies, whenever their interests converged. On this trip, Kissinger was playing second fiddle to Nixon, who was making his first and desperately awaited trip to China. Being the President, Nixon, seated in the President's Guest House in Beijing, explained to Zhou the viewpoint of his country with regard to the subcontinent: 'I should emphasise our policy is not anti-Indian any more than the Prime Minister's policy is anti-Indian. It's pro-peace. It is the right of every nation in the subcontinent to survive and develop. This right should be recognized and protected, and if one country should be allowed to gobble up another, it would be a very unsafe world. We apply that to every country, including ourselves.'

To this, Premier Zhou Enlai replied: 'It would be another question if the people of that country rise up themselves to change the government. It is quite another thing if foreign troops invade a country. That can't be allowed. That's a very important principle.'[31]

Nixon spoke of his policy towards India (his tilt toward Pakistan was already well-known): 'The Indian decisions were mine. If anything, again speaking to the Prime

Minister in the confidence we always use, we made two mistakes. The first of these I could do nothing about—not seeing that Pakistan had enough arms to discourage an Indian attack. Secondly, when I saw Mrs. Gandhi I made a mistake in listening to my advisers, who said to reassure her. So I spent the whole time reassuring her when I should have warned her. So I'm the hard-liner on India. I must say he (Dr. Kissinger) was a conspirator with me. We agreed on that policy.'[32]

During the course of this third round of discussions, focusing on the situation in South Asia, Premier Zhou covered areas of potential discord such as the withdrawal of Indian troops to within their own international boundaries, as they had done unilaterally in 1962. ('One must show one can be trusted and must not wait for others to act.') He was prepared to recognise the new state of Bangladesh after the implementation of the UN resolutions regarding troop withdrawals ('We will probably recognize Bangladesh later on. Perhaps we will be the last one.') He regarded Kashmir as being 'something Great Britain deliberately left behind' and cautioned against the possibility of India thinking that the problem of Kashmir had been solved with the cease-fire. And in a perceptive analogy, he compared the ethnic diversity of India with that of the US: 'From our point of view, even if the subcontinent were under one country there would still be turmoil there, because they have nationality problems there even more complicated than yours which are now covered up. If India took over all of the subcontinent, there would be even more trouble.'[33]

Both Nixon and Zhou found that they shared a low opinion of Mrs Gandhi. To Sultan Khan, Zhou had once mentioned that he could not understand why the 'faint-hearted' Prime Minister of such a large country could not find the time to call on her larger neighbour.[34] To Nixon, he disclosed: 'Even before the India-Pakistan conflict, we were contemplating returning our ambassador to India. We wanted to improve our relations with India. The Indian government expressed a desire for that, too. Madame Gandhi published this.'

Nixon replied: 'She told me that when I saw her in New Delhi and in Washington. But she also told me some other things, too. (Prime Minister laughs.) She said she would not oppose my meetings with the Prime Minister and the Chinese government, just don't harm her.'

'Don't harm her ...' Zhou Enlai retorted, 'who wants to harm her?'[35]

And when, at the end of their talks, just as Nixon and his wife Pat were leaving to board their plane at Shanghai, President Nixon mentioned 'on a less serious note' that the press had reported a statement by Mrs Gandhi on his visit to China, Premier Zhou replied, "I don't think that is very serious, and we won't take it seriously."

"Yes, but..." interjected Dr. Kissinger.

Premier Zhou closed the subject with: "Although she is so big a state, I think that this manouver is very petty."[36]

If Nixon and Zhou shared a common opinion of Mrs Gandhi, they shared an uncommonly high one of President Yahya Khan—the bridge who had brought them together. Zhou Enlai spoke of him as being 'probably a good man, a man of good intentions, but he did not know how to lead an army, how to fight. So there was some reason for the dissatisfaction of the younger generals in the Pakistani army with President Yahya, but there is also some reason to say good words about him. I agree with that spirit.

President Nixon concurred: 'As Dr. Kissinger said in his conversation with the Prime Minister, one doesn't burn a bridge which has proved useful'.

Zhou replied: 'Yes there is a saying that to tear down a bridge after having crossed it is in not good.'

During the same conversation, Dr Kissinger mentioned to Zhou Enlai that 'the President sent a message to Bhutto that he should treat Yahya well in retirement and we should not look favorably on any retribution. It was a personal message from the President.'

Zhou replied laconically: 'He [Bhutto] also told us that he was taking good care of him and protecting him, and that if he didn't do so, some of the other generals would want to take care of him (Yahya) differently.'[37] The sense of obligation these three—Nixon, Kissinger and Zhou Enlai—felt towards Yahya was not so much for his person as for the role he had played in helping bring to fruition an abstract policy they had initiated without the knowledge of the very people whose interest they were serving.

That they needed to conduct their diplomacy in the strictest of secrecy, placed them in a unique dilemma; that most dangerous of moral dilemmas, as Dag Hammarskjold, a former UN secretary-general,[38] had once written, '...when we are obliged to conceal truth in order to help the truth to be victorious.'[39]

To succeed they had to use unconventional methods, stratagems which were unorthodox, and at times resort to subterfuge. Each, like the nineteenth century Austrian diplomat Prince Klemens von Metternich, could justify being 'devious, because the very certainty of his convictions made him entirely flexible in his choice of means.' Perhaps not surprisingly, that last quotation comes from a doctoral thesis on Metternich and his British counterpart Lord Castlereagh submitted to Harvard University in 1954 by a graduate student whose name happened to be Henry A. Kissinger.[40]

Despite or because of Kissinger's insistence on secrecy, Nixon, he and the inner core of trusted intermediaries were not the only ones to know of his furtive trip to Beijing in July 1971. While Kissinger had found it necessary to set up a secure channel through the office of the Naval Attaché in Karachi, copies of his cypher messages were being relayed back to Secretary Defense Melvin Laird and Admiral Elmo R. Zumwalt, Jr.[41]

In addition, the Pentagon secreted a Navy yeoman, Charles Radford, as a stenographer into Henry Kissinger's office. Radford's mission was to obtain documents and then, after copying them, to send those copies to the Joint Chiefs of Staff at the Pentagon.[42] One of the documents Radford managed to obtain from Kissinger's briefcase was Kissinger's personal memo of his conversations with Zhou Enlai during their first secret meeting in July 1971.[43] This too was copied and sent to the Pentagon.

That even such a privileged document should have been accessed was perhaps to be expected, keeping in mind the furtive nature of the whole secret channel enterprise. It was almost certainly the most significant document of its kind in twentieth century diplomatic history to be purloined in such a manner, by an American of an American for an American.

NOTES

1. The 'sanitised' version—a tenth of the original—was sent from the White House by General Alexander Haig, as Kissinger's Deputy Assistant to the President for National Security Affairs, to Theodore Eliot, Executive Secretary, State Department, on 28 January 1972. I am grateful to Mr William Burr for this reference.

2. *Memorandum of Conversation No. 2*, 22 February 1972 (National Security Archive, Washington).
3. Sisson and Rose (1990), p. 295, note 21.
4. Nixon (1978), p. 525.
5. Kissinger (1979), p. 739.
6. Chief of the General Staff, Pakistan Army (December 1968– December 1971).
7. Khan (1997), pp. 303–4.
8. Khan (1997), pp. 307–8.
9. Nikita S. Khrushchev (Soviet Premier, 1958–64). He died in 1971.
10. *Memorandum for The President from Henry A. Kissinger*, 17 July 1971, pp. 17–18. Record Group 59, Dept. of State Records, 1970–73.
11. Burr (1998), p. 482.
12. Khan (1997), p. 243.
13. Quoted also in Khan (1997), p. 269.
14. Khan (1997), p. 307.
15. Kissinger (1979), p. 767. Kissinger noted that 'repeatedly during my conversations with Chou En-lai a deep and abiding Chinese hatred of the Russians came through. The Chinese are concerned about Soviet power, but utterly contemptuous of the motivations of the leaders who exercise this power.' *Memorandum for The President from Henry A. Kissinger*, 29 October 1971, p. 7. Record Group 59, Dept. of State Records, 1970–73.
16. *Memorandum for The President from Henry A. Kissinger*, 11 November 1971, pp. 26–27. Record Group 59, Dept. of State Records, 1970–73.
17. Ibid., p. 5.
18. Nixon (1982), p. 271.
19. Nixon (1982), p. 273.
20. Marshal Chen Yi, Deputy Premier of the China State Council and for a time Foreign Minister.
21. *Memorandum of Conversation No. 3*, 23 February 1972, p. 10 (National Security Archive, Washington).
22. Nixon (1978), p. 525.
23. Kissinger (1979), p. 878.
24. Jayakar (1995), p. 233.
25. Mrs Gandhi's reference was to the Pathan leader Khan Abdul Ghaffar Khan (1890–1988), known to the Indians as the Frontier Gandhi.

26. Kissinger (1979), p. 881.
27. Kissinger (1979), p. 896.
28. Burr (1998), p. 52.
29. Burr (1998), pp. 54–5.
30. Kissinger (1979), p. 913.
31. *Memorandum of Conversation No. 3*, 23 February 1972, p. 11 (National Security Archive, Washington).
32. *Memorandum of Conversation No. 3*, 23 February 1972, p. 22 (National Security Archive, Washington).
33. *Memorandum of Conversation No. 3*, 23 February 1972, p. 6 (National Security Archive, Washington).
34. Khan (1997), p. 177.
35. *Memorandum of Conversation No. 4*, 24 February, 1972, p. 29 (National Security Archive, Washington).
36. *Memorandum of Conversation No. 7*, 28 February 1972, p. 11 (National Security Archive, Washington).
37. *Memorandum of Conversation No. 3*, 23 February 1972, pp. 7 and 8 (National Security Archive, Washington).
38. Dag Hammarskjold, Secretary General UN (1953–61). Awarded the Nobel Peace Prize posthumously in 1961.
39. This quotation, published in Kissinger (1979), p. 763, was sent to him by William Safire, Nixon's speech-writer (1969–73).
40. Isaacson (1993), p. 77.
41. Isaacson (1993), p. 201.
42. Isaacson (1993), p. 298.
43. Nixon (1978), pp. 531–2.

APPENDIX A

Record of a discussion between Gen Sher Ali Khan and
Mr Henry Kissinger at the White House on Friday 10th
October 1969. TOP SECRET.

Gen Sher Ali said that President Yahya Khan had wanted
him to tell Mr Kissinger that he would like to be of assistance in regard to the U.S.-Chinese problem but would
like to know on what lines he should discuss the matter at
the top level with the Chinese. President Yahya would of
course take the line that Nixon would like to normalise
American relations with Peking but it should be obvious
to the Chinese that this would take some time as it had to
be effected gradually since American public opinion had
to prepared carefully for the change. The General added
that the Chinese would then want to know what measures
the Americans were prepared to take as concrete proof of
such an intention.

Mr Kissinger said he agreed President Yahya should be
briefed on specific points for this purpose. He (Kissinger)
could give us an idea of the general lines on which we
could negotiate with the Chinese but he would do some
more thinking on this matter & would prefer to communi-
cate the result to Ambassador Hilaly in a few day's time.
(Evidently he wanted to consult President Nixon first.) In
any case Chou En Lai was not coming to Pakistan till
January.

Kissinger continued that immediately however we could tell the Chinese that U.S. is withdrawing the two destroyers which are patrolling the Formosa Straits and are irksome to the Chinese. This should help the atmosphere and assist us in our talks even though it was a very small measure. By doing so, however, U.S. was not altering its position re Formosa or anything else at this stage.

Gen Sher Ali asked whether we should convey this information to the Chinese through our Ambassador at Peking or through the Chinese Ambassador in Islamabad. Mr Kissinger replied that secrecy was vital in these matters & he would much prefer if President Yahya Khan could kindly deal with the Chinese Ambassador himself without anybody else being present. It was essential to keep both State Dept. and the Pakistan Foreign Office out of this affair.

Mr Kissinger next enquired whether President Yahya Khan had asked Gen Abdul Hamid Khan to discuss this matter with the Chinese leaders during his recent visit to Peking for the 1st October celebrations. Gen Sher Ali replied that he did not know as he had been away from Pakistan since middle of September. He promised, however, he would find out on his return to Islamabad and would inform Mr Kissinger through Ambassador Hilaly.

[For text reference, see page no. 28]

APPENDIX B

COMMENTS OF WARREN UNNA, ON WETA/TV
NEWS PANEL PROGRAM, OCTOBER 6, 1970. (From
unofficial notes)

In the program's brief introductory sequence, Unna stated
he had a "scoop" that the U.S. is about to sell planes and
armored personnel carriers to Pakistan, thereby ending the
five-year embargo on arms sale to India and Pakistan.

When called on later in the program, Unna reported that
"President Nixon apparently has personally decided to sell
Pakistan old U.S. B-57 bombers, F-104 fighter jets and
armored personnel carriers at marked down military so-
called surplus rates." He gave the cost as about $15 million,
but said this makes little sense when one squadron of F-
104s cost much more than that.

"The President made this decision—or at least it was
underway—in June and it was personally taken in hand by
Mr. Nixon. I am told he pencilled in the B-57 bombers
himself and he apparently was heavily persuaded by
Pakistan's Ambassador here, Agha Hilaly, who was very
persuasive.

"The announcement was held up, and as a matter of fact
they have no intention of announcing it, but sometimes
these things get out as it did to me and it was. The Senate

Foreign Relations Committee was told about 10 days ago
and the Indians were given a forewarning, just a very vague
idea, about a week ago."

[For text reference, see page no. 38]

BIBLIOGRAPHY

Aijazuddin, F.S., 'From a Head, through a Head to a Head', *The Armless Queen and Other Essays* (Lahore, 1994).

Akhund, Iqbal, *Memoirs of a Bystander. A Life in Diplomacy* (Karachi, 1997).

Area Handbook for Pakistan (Washington, 1965).

Bhutto, Benazir, *Daughter of the East* (London, 1988).

Bhutto, Zulfikar A., *Bilateralism. New Directions* (Islamabad, 1976).

Burney, I.H., *No Illusions, Some Hopes and No Fears. The Outlook Editorials of I.H. Burney 1962-4; 1972-4* (Karachi, 1996).

Burr, William (ed.), *The Kissinger Transcripts. The Top Secret talks with Beijing and Moscow* (New York, 1998).

Feldman, Herbert, *The End and the Beginning: Pakistan 1969-1971* (London, 1975; reprinted Karachi, 1976).

Gartoff, Raymond L., *Détente and Confrontation. American-Soviet Relations from Nixon to Reagan.* (Washington, 1994).

Gauhar, Altaf, *Ayub Khan. Pakistan's First Military Ruler* (Lahore, 1993).

Gopal, Sarvepalli, *Jawaharlal Nehru: a biography* (Delhi, 1979).

Gromyko, Andrei, *Memories* Translated by H. Shukman. (London, 1989).

Holdridge, John H., *Crossing the Divide: An Insider's Account of the Normalization of U.S.-China Relations* (Lanham, USA/Oxford, 1997).

Isaacson, Walter, *Kissinger. A Biography* (London, 1992; 1993 edition).

James, Sir Morrice (Lord Saint Brides), *Pakistan Chronicle* (Karachi, 1993).

Jayakar, Pupul, *Indira Gandhi: A biography* (Delhi, 1992; edition 1995).

Khan, Sultan M., *Memories & Reflections of a Pakistani Diplomat* (London, 1997).

Kissinger, Henry, *White House Years* (Boston, 1979).

_____, *Years of Upheaval* (London, 1982).

Li, Dr. Zhisui, *The Private Life of Chairman Mao: The Memoirs of Mao's Personal Physician* (New York, 1994; 1996 edition).

Mann, James, *About Face. A history of America's curious relationship with China, from Nixon to Clinton.* (New York, 1999).

Nehru, B. K., *Nice Guys Finish Second* (New Delhi, 1997).

Nixon, Richard, *The Memoirs of Richard Nixon* (New York, 1978).

_____, *Leaders* (London, 1982).

Pakistan Year Book (Annual editions 1969 to 1981).

Raza, Rafi, *Zulfikar Ali Bhutto and Pakistan 1967-1977* (Karachi, 1997).

Sisson, Richard and Rose, Leo E., *War and Secession: Pakistan, India and the creation of Bangladesh* (California, 1990; OUP Karachi, 1992).

Suhrawardy, *Memoirs of Huseyn Shaheed Suhrawardy.* Edited by M.H.R. Talukdar. (Dhaka, 1987).

Twenty Years of Pakistan. Introduction by Altaf Gauhar. (Karachi, 1967).

Tyler, Patrick, *A Great Wall. Six Presidents and China: an investigative history.* (New York, 1999).

Williams, L. F. Rushbrook, *The State of Pakistan* (London, 1962).

Wolpert, Stanley, *Zulfi Bhutto of Pakistan* (Karachi, 1993).

INDEX